The Moneymaker

JANET GLEESON

Level 5

Retold by Eryl Griffiths
Series Editors: Andy Hopkins and Jocelyn Potter

Pearson Education Limited
Edinburgh Gate, Harlow,
Essex CM20 2JE, England
and Associated Companies throughout the world.

ISBN 0 582 45353 4

First published in the UK by Bantam Press 1999
This edition first published by Penguin 2001

Original copyright © Janet Gleeson 1999
Text copyright © Penguin Books 2001
The moral rights of the author have been asserted

Typeset by Ferdinand Pageworks, London
Set in 11/14pt Bembo
Printed in Spain by Mateu Cromo, S. A. Pinto (Madrid)

Published by Pearson Education Limited in association with
Penguin Books Ltd, both companies being subsidiaries of Pearson Plc

For a complete list of the titles available in the Penguin Readers series please write to your local
Pearson Education office or to: Marketing Department, Penguin Longman Publishing,
80 Strand, London WC2R 0RL.

Contents

Introduction

'I do not pretend that I have not made mistakes . . . and if I could start again . . . I would go more slowly but more carefully.'

Three hundred years ago, wealth in most Western countries was stored and exchanged in the form of gold and silver coins. There were never enough. Never enough to pay for the wars and the rich lifestyles of kings, never enough to expand business and industry.

John Law was a charming Edinburgh Scot who was brilliant with numbers and made a fortune from gambling on his travels round Europe. But he had more than one reason for travelling. He had killed a man in a duel, he had escaped from prison, he had run off with another man's wife. .

Law arrived in Paris with an idea – paper money. He worked hard to gain political support and to start the first French bank which printed paper notes. At the height of his success he created a trading company. Shareholders made enormous profits and the word 'millionaire' was invented to describe them.

Then things went wrong. People lost confidence in the paper money and there was panic. Fortunes were lost as quickly as they had been made. Law had many enemies and he was forced to escape from France – sadder, wiser, and much, much poorer. But when we see world business today using plastic cards and paper cheques, with no gold or silver in sight, it is clear that John Law's dream has come true.

Janet Gleeson was born in Sri Lanka, where her father was a tea grower. She studied the History of Art and English, and in 1991 she started working for a publisher, Reed Books. She has also written *Miller's Antiques and Collectibles* and *The Arcanum*.

Chapter 1 Young John Law

John Law's family background does not suggest the professional gambler, murderer, adventurer and international banker that he later became. For many years the Laws had followed careers in the Church of Scotland, and John Law's grandfather was a minister in the little village of Neilston in Renfrewshire until, in 1649, he lost his job and was forced to take the family to Edinburgh in search of employment. Edinburgh was not the beautiful city that we know today. At that time it was poor, crowded and dirty and was only just recovering from the worst plague in its history. Minister Law and his family had a hard life.

Since the early sixteenth century, members of the Law family who were not involved in the Church had worked as goldsmiths, and so John Law's father, William, and his brother were sent to learn this profession. They were taught how to make jewellery and other objects from gold, and also to work as money dealers. Gold and silver were the main forms of money in those days, and the most successful goldsmiths had great power and wealth and a high social position.

By 1661, young William had finished his training and had started his own business. He lived in the commercial district of the city in a tall, narrow building which housed his shop and workshop on the ground floor and the family rooms upstairs. He married, but his first wife died within a year and in 1663 he married Jean Campbell, the daughter of a rich businessman. With her money he bought a second shop. William and Jean Law had twelve children, but only four lived beyond childhood. John was their fifth child and the oldest son. He was born in April 1671, probably in one of the tiny rooms above the goldsmith's shop.

By this time, William Law had become a top goldsmith,

responsible for the testing of all the gold and silver objects made in the city. He was as ambitious for his children as for himself and he sent John to the Edinburgh High School, where the boy studied religion, mathematics, Latin and perhaps modern languages. John was a clever child and particularly good with numbers.

John Law grew up in a rapidly changing city. Edinburgh had grown richer; it had new gardens, street lighting, coffee houses and a new Exchange. At home he was surrounded by money-making deals and watched the workers that his father employed making beautiful objects of gold and silver.

In 1683, William Law bought Lauriston Castle and some land outside the city. But before the family could move there, tragedy struck. After years of hard work, William fell ill and went to Paris for an operation. He never recovered and was buried in the Scots College in Paris. His wife Jean had to care for the family and to look after their finances. Lauriston Castle was left to John, then twelve years old, but with money that his father had left for his education John was sent away from the city to school. There he continued his studies and also learned sword-fighting and tennis.

John Law grew into a handsome and popular young man who developed interests in fine clothes, gambling and women. He enjoyed the risk-taking of gambling as much, if not more, than the money. Women found him attractive, charming and humorous. He passed his time pleasurably, avoided hard work and chose not to go to university. Soon, though, he began to dream of a world beyond Edinburgh; he wanted to experience London, which at that time was ten days' journey away. His mother agreed to let him go, hoping perhaps that he would find work there.

London was an enormous city of 750,000 people, the largest Western European capital and a very exciting place for a young man to be. Since the Great Fire of 1666, a lot of new buildings had been put up. To the north and east there were factories and workshops surrounded by the pitiful homes of the poorest workers. To the west the aristocrats and businessmen lived in grand houses among green fields.

Law settled in St Giles, a fashionable suburb of London which included Holborn, Covent Garden, Seven Dials and Bloomsbury. At that time it was almost a village. Law's desire to be accepted into London 'society' took him to theatres, St James's Park and Vauxhall Gardens. He ate in fashionable pubs and visited famous coffee houses. He spent his money foolishly on gambling and women. Gambling gave him a way into society, and women provided relaxation from its demands and disappointments. At some time after his arrival in London, he was joined in his rooms by a mysterious woman called Mrs Lawrence. Little is known of her, but she played an important part in his future career.

Not surprisingly, by 1692 – and before his twenty-first birthday – Law had spent or lost all his money. If he could not pay his debts, he would be put in prison, so he had to ask his mother to sell Lauriston Castle. Fortunately she was a sensible person who had looked after her own money well. She was able to buy the castle and land from him and so save her son from shame and from prison while keeping the money in the family.

This changed Law's attitude to gambling. He was a proud and private person and he hated asking his mother for help. He understood now how easily he could lose everything at the card tables. But it was impossible not to gamble – everyone in society did it. To reduce the risk, without losing the excitement, he began to look for ways of increasing his chances of winning.

Many important scientists like Geralamo Cardano at Padua University, Galileo, and the mathematicians Pascal and Jakob Bernoulli, had studied probability theory. John Law read books on the subject and easily learned this 'science of chance'. He taught himself to calculate, at great speed, the probability of the appearance of a certain card. His system worked and Law's luck changed. Betting became a serious business for him.

He often took the role of 'banker' in card games to improve his chances of winning, and he only bet heavily when he was sure that his chances were good. He also invented his own gambling games. And his study of probability led him to one of the new interests of his time: the science of economics.

◆

Money has always been a problem. For rich and poor, there is never enough. In the late seventeenth century, the problem was desperate. Money was gold and silver and these had to be found and dug out of the ground. The supply could not meet the demand. The population of Europe was growing, kings had spent their money on long and terrible wars, money was needed for new businesses at home and abroad. The main question of the day was how to make more money. Some people still looked for the magic that could turn ordinary metals into gold, while bankers, businessmen and politicians began to use paper notes and shares. These, too, seemed like magic to many people.

Money, economists tell us, is a way to make exchange easier. If we did not have money, we could only exchange things – eggs for oranges, carpets for bricks, a book for a bowl of rice. At different times and in different places many things have been used as money – cows, wives, tobacco, shells. But gold and silver have been used for longer and in more places.

Banking is a very old profession. The first bankers lived 3,000 years ago in Babylon.* There were bankers in Athens in 500 BC who changed money for foreign visitors. And in Rome money-lending bankers were powerful people. The first modern banks were in Italian cities like Genoa, Turin, Pisa and Milan in the Middle Ages.† The word 'bank' comes from the Italian word

---

* Babylon: the ancient capital city of the country that is now Iraq.
† The Middle Ages: the years from AD 1000 to AD 1500.

banco, meaning the seat where the money-dealers sat. But the problem was always the same: there was not enough gold and silver for people's needs, hopes, dreams and plans.

J. K. Galbraith, a famous modern economist, says the idea of credit changed the situation. If gold and silver were kept in safety in a bank, the owner could take away a piece of paper to prove that the money was his. Then the bankers could lend some of the gold and silver to other people, charging interest and making a profit. In this way money would be multiplied and the problem of not having enough gold and silver would be solved. The only trouble was if an outside event made everyone want their gold and silver back at the same time, then the bank would be unable to pay them and the system would be bankrupt. A calm political situation and large amounts of metal money in the banks were needed for the system of credit and paper money to work.

Britain was slow to use credit. People thought money-lending for profit was a crime against God and such 'criminals' used to be hanged. In the Middle Ages first Jews, and later Italian goldsmiths known as Lombards, were allowed to lend money. The Italians had to live and work in one street in London, Lombard Street. This street is still today at the heart of international financial dealing. By the middle of the seventeenth century, laws against money-lending were relaxed but banking remained a risky business.

Chapter 2   The Duel

As their carriage drew into Bloomsbury Square, the two men saw John Law waiting. Perhaps he heard the carriage, and turned to watch as one of them got out and walked purposefully towards him. It was just past midday on 9 April 1694.

Bloomsbury Square was on the edge of London. Three sides

had large, new houses for rich people but the other side had open fields full of flowers and fruit trees. It was a favourite place for couples in love and a favourite place for fighting duels. Here John Law waited nervously as the man from the carriage approached. It seems – according to several witnesses – that they had arranged a meeting. As the man came face to face with John, perhaps drunk and over-confident, he pulled out his sword. Immediately and, Law said later, without thinking, Law reacted. Pulling out his sword – 'a weapon of iron and steel' – with surprising speed, Law struck a single, defensive blow. With a short, desperate cry, his enemy fell, dead, to the ground.

History does not record what happened next. We can guess, however, that a crowd formed, and that among the crowd was an officer of the law. John seems to have made no attempt to escape. Answering the officer's questions, he said that he was twenty-three and lived in St Giles, where he had settled several years ago after moving from Edinburgh. The officer turned to the dead man and his friend, who introduced himself as Captain Wightman. The dead man, noted the officer, was of similar age to John Law and grandly dressed. He was Edward Wilson, one of London's most famous and mysterious young men in high society. He would be talked about even more now he was dead.

Wilson's father was a poor Leicester gentleman. Wilson himself had been an ordinary soldier in Flanders in his youth, but recently he had lived such a wild life in London that he had become famous. He had paid off his father's debts and taken care of his sisters by introducing them into society, where he hoped they would find good husbands. He dressed and lived like the richest aristocrat. He had a fine house with beautiful furniture. He had many servants and a carriage pulled by six horses. No man entertained more generously or paid better. But where had the money come from? No one knew. And no one knew when he had first quarrelled with John Law.

One of Edward's sisters had moved into the house where John lived with Mrs Lawrence, and Wilson and Law had quarrelled. Wilson wrote angry letters about Law's living arrangements, and things got worse when Miss Wilson left and found rooms somewhere else. Law wrote angry letters to Wilson and finally visited him in his grand house. Over a drink, he warned Wilson to stop spreading stories about himself and Mrs Lawrence.

But the trouble continued. On the morning of 9 April 1694, Law entered the Fountain bar in the Strand and came face to face with Wilson and his friend Captain Wightman. They talked, but we do not know what they actually said. We only know that from there they made their separate ways to Bloomsbury and the duel.

John Law was taken to Newgate prison, a terrible place as we know from the writer Daniel Defoe's description in his novel *Moll Flanders*. Luckily Law had money and friends in high places, so he was able to get a cell away from the worst terrors and dirt of the area where the common criminals were kept. Law's friends wanted him to deny his part in the duel, but he would not. His story never changed: Wilson pulled out his sword first, Law had acted in self-defence. But in the eyes of a seventeenth-century court, the question was not who had started the duel but whether it had been arranged – and so Law had planned to kill Wilson. The letters between the two men were found and Law was accused of murder.

Sir Salathiel Lovell was the judge. This terrible old man with an awful memory always imprisoned or hanged as many people as he could, unless they were willing to pay him not to. Law, by now just twenty-three, had never been in court before and believed he would get a fair trial. Faced with Lovell's 'justice', he was disappointed. It seems likely that both judge and jury had been paid by Wilson's powerful relatives. Law was found guilty of murder and would be hanged.

After the shocks of the duel and the trial, Law could only wait to see what would happen. He was surprisingly calm. In high society, in those days, duelling was a custom among gentlemen if they felt they had been insulted. Usually the King would pardon a duellist. 'I neither heard before nor after that killing a man in a fair duel was found murder' said Law's aristocratic friend, James Johnston. So Law probably expected to be pardoned and felt no cause for alarm.

But Wilson's cousins wanted revenge and they were close to King William. They guessed that Law's friends would ask the King for a royal pardon, so they acted quickly to persuade him that Law was not a gentleman and had planned to murder their cousin. Caught in the middle, the King was upset and did not want to discuss the matter at all. But Johnston was a true friend and supporter of Law's, and risked the King's anger many times by trying to explain his case. The King, however, believed that the duel had not been a question of honour but a quarrel about money; this is why he would not pardon John Law.

Johnston asked the Duke of Shrewsbury for help and the Duke advised him to be patient, to wait for the King to calm down, and at the same time to look for proof that money was not the cause of the quarrel. Johnston discovered that just before the duel Law had received £400 from Scotland, so he had not been short of money. Shrewsbury presented this proof to the King, but the King had already promised Wilson's cousins that he would not pardon Law unless they agreed. Under pressure from both sides, the King finally decided not to hang Law but to keep him in prison.

Law was moved to Southwark prison, and a new trial with a new judge began two months later. Law now had good lawyers, but the Wilsons' legal team had prepared a very strong case against him. Public opinion and even his closest friends felt that he was going to lose. The case was complicated, and the judge decided to delay his decision until the autumn.

Law faced spending the summer in the horrible prison of Southwark; horrible, but not difficult to get out of. His friends had been trying to persuade him to escape, and finally he listened to them. Tools were secretly brought in to him, and by mid-October he was filing down the bars of his prison cell and dreaming of freedom. But his guards caught him on 20 October and, to prevent any further attempts at escape, he was chained up. Then the judge decided against Law and a trial date was set for the new year, 1695. Everything had gone wrong, and even his best friend Johnston said, 'I am afraid Mr Law shall be hanged at last.'

The events that followed are a mystery, and we cannot tell fact from fiction. The usual story, which Law never discouraged, is that somehow he got tools and drugs. Just before his trial, he broke free of his chains, drugged his guards, filed down the bars of his cell, climbed the prison wall – and suffered only a twisted ankle in the process. A waiting carriage took him to the coast, and he sailed to safety on the Continent.*

The truth was almost certainly more complicated, and much more amazing. By autumn 1694, it seemed that Law was sure to hang, but his friends had not forgotten him. They still tried to present his case to the King. The King finally decided that the best way out of the problem would be for Law to escape. In total secrecy the King told the Duke of Shrewsbury, and Shrewsbury told Johnston.

Johnston reacted quickly, finding two men to drug the guards and help Law escape. Johnston kept the secret and never spoke of the matter while the King and the Duke lived. Law himself never really knew what happened. When the two men arrived in his cell, he thought at first that it was a trick of the Wilsons', but the men worked quickly and soon had him free.

When the escape was announced a few days later in the King's

* the Continent: the continent of Europe (not including Britain).

court, the Wilsons were extremely angry. They attempted to find Law, and offered a reward to anyone who could catch him. A description of Law with an offer of a fifty-pound reward was published in a newspaper, the *London Gazette*, on Monday 7 January 1695. But the Duke of Shrewsbury produced this newspaper and somehow the description of John Law which it printed was quite inaccurate.

The public talked about the duel and the escape for years. Many strange theories were suggested for Wilson's mysterious supply of money and about the quarrel between him and Law. Wilson had often claimed that, however long he lived, he had enough money to continue his grand lifestyle. The book *The Unknown Lady's Pacquet of Letters* which was published in 1707 offered one solution. The author claimed that Wilson had met a mysterious woman in Kensington Gardens and, without knowing who she was, had started a relationship with her. The woman forced Wilson to agree that he would never attempt to find out who she was, and had paid him a generous salary. But Wilson was curious and did not keep his promise. When he discovered that the woman was Elizabeth Villiers, the King's unattractive lover, she was angry that he had broken his promise and she asked Law, who was a friend of hers, to take revenge for them both. She promised Law that she would persuade the King not to punish him.

This extraordinary story was matched about ten years later by another little book. It claimed that Wilson's money came secretly from a male lover, and that Law had been involved in the matter and had quarrelled with Wilson about that. But by the time this story was published, in 1723, Law was an internationally famous figure who had changed finance in the western world. Europe was full of attacks on his character and background – and this, probably, was just one of them. The truth remains unclear.

However, the duel, the trials and the escape show a pattern

which we see again and again in John Law's life. His high principles and refusal to change, his willingness to risk everything – life itself – in a matter of honour later placed him in similar situations, when he had to trust powerful friends to save him. We do not know if it was the duelling custom or a wild courage which made him fight Wilson in the first place. But the violence of the duel, the closeness to death and the horrors of prison certainly upset him more than he showed. Years later, these painful memories perhaps caused the loss of control that he suffered in similar tense situations.

Certainly, too, the mysterious John Law had decided that the duel's full story should not be told. As he stood on the ship crossing to the Continent and enjoyed his freedom, he forgot his past and prepared for a new life.

Chapter 3   Love in Exile

We do not know exactly what Law did after leaving London. He appeared in France, gambling at high society parties. He spent time in prison in Caen – his papers were not in order. He also visited Holland and various cities in Italy. Everywhere he went, his life followed a familiar pattern, with gambling and dangerous relationships with women as the main events. But John Law was also developing his interest in economics.

We can see this by the places he visited: Amsterdam, Venice, Genoa and Turin had cultural and social attractions. All were cities with plenty of rich tourists and citizens, where a gambler of Law's ability could be sure of an income. In addition, all were important financial centres. Amsterdam, his home for several years, was like a large garden, with good roads shaded on each side by rows of trees; it had fine public buildings, beautiful houses, and women 'more nicely clean' than the English. But Law liked the city because it was the commercial capital of Europe, and its success was due to a bank.

♦

In the financial confusion of the time, the Bank of Amsterdam had achieved the impossible: the country's economy was healthy, trade grew, and for a time the Netherlands was the most powerful commercial nation in the world. The bank was started in 1609, and its principles were simple. Bad coins were a serious problem in Continental Europe, as they were in England, and a great variety – about 800 different types of gold and silver coins – were in use. Coins could be exchanged in every town and market in Europe, but in Amsterdam the bank took local and foreign coins, weighed and tested them, and in return gave credit notes or bank money – a kind of paper money – equal to their real, metal value. The bank money, Law observed, had great advantages. It made payments easier and quicker, the bank saved the costs of transport and losses from bad money, and the money was safe from fire and robbery. The bank guaranteed the credit notes and the state guaranteed the bank. The public preferred the paper money to metal coins and the notes were usually exchanged for more than their stated value.

Amsterdam's bank was not the first to use paper money. Paper notes were invented, like so many clever things, by the Chinese, who used them in the seventh century. In Europe, nearly a thousand years later, a Swede called Johan Palmstruch was given royal permission to start a private bank in 1656, in return for giving half his profits to the King. Sweden had other metals but very little gold or silver. Its money included enormous metal sheets weighing as much as fifteen kilograms – so heavy that people carried them on their backs or used horses to transport them. In 1661, Palmstruch and his Stockholm *banco* stopped this inconvenience by printing paper money equal in value to the

12

metal sheets – the first true European banknotes as we understand them today. Things went well at first but Palmstruch printed too many notes. Six years later, he could not exchange the paper for gold or silver and the bank was bankrupt. Palmstruch was sent to prison and only just escaped hanging.

Thirty years later, in America, paper money was tried again. In 1690 the Massachusetts Bay Colony was forced to pay its soldiers with banknotes because it did not have coins. The soldiers were promised that they could exchange their notes for coins when the local people had paid their taxes. But two years later, the Colony was still so short of coins that the paper money was made official.

Amsterdam was the shining example of cautious lending among all the different and disastrous attempts to introduce paper money. Lending to private individuals was carefully controlled; there was no printing of notes without a high percentage of metal kept at the bank to guarantee them. As a result, everyone trusted the bank. Foreigners kept their money there. English, Spanish and other governments used the bank. It lent money for low interest, and so ships were built and trade increased. In 1609, the bank had 730 accounts; by the end of the century, it had 2,700. Trust in a bank had guaranteed a whole nation's fortune.

♦

In 1697, two years after Law's life of exile began, the bitter Nine Years War between France, Austria, Holland, England, Spain, Sweden and Savoy ended, and it became easier to travel round Europe. This is probably the time when Law made his first visit to Paris. Louis XIV had been king for forty years, and during this time Paris had become one of the most beautiful cities in Europe.

In Paris gambling was even more popular than in England, and when he had settled Law soon joined the games at the high society parties. One friend remembered that Law never carried less than two bags filled with gold coins. Perhaps it was after a particularly successful evening at the tables that he was introduced to Madame★ Katherine Seigneur, an aristocratic English woman who had married a Frenchman. She was well-dressed and rather handsome, with a proud and difficult character.

Although in England intelligent women were not popular – most men agreed with Samuel Johnson's joke that a man is happier when he has a good dinner on the table than when his wife speaks Greek – in France it was different. In Parisian society women enjoyed more independence. Law had learned to respect his mother's business skills and perhaps this clever woman reminded him of her. Anyway, he showed an interest in her and she, obviously dissatisfied with her marriage, encouraged him. Even if she had not been married, such a relationship would have been a problem; she was an aristocrat and he was a gambler. But Law and Katherine were far from home and their families, and they did what they wanted. Certainly, Katherine's husband (about whom we know nothing except his name) made no objections – probably because he was absent when she and Law met.

At the same time, Law's successes at the gambling tables had some unfortunate but unsurprising results. People did not want to play against him because he won so often. He was suspected of cheating. The time had come for him to move on; only Katherine kept him in Paris. In their high society world, affairs were common and could be quickly forgotten, however unsuitable. But Law and Katherine did not just have a secret affair. They left Paris together; they were publicly committed to each other. The story of their escape was on the front pages of the Paris newspapers.

They went to Italy, the birthplace of European banking; first to Genoa, and then later to Rome, Florence, Turin and Venice. In each city he visited, Law played the gambling tables and worked

★ *Madame, Monsieur, Mademoiselle*: the French words for *Mrs, Mr, Miss*.

on his financial theories. In Venice he went constantly to the state bank, the Rialto, when the exchange was open and watched the international deals. He saw how useful paper credit was and how the bank made its profits.

By the end of his tour of Italy Law had made many important friends, including the Dukes of Savoy and Vendôme. He now had financial knowledge and £20,000 made from gambling, money-lending and foreign exchange trading. But he was dissatisfied. Perhaps ambition meant that it was not enough for him to make money for himself. Perhaps they were tired of travelling and Katherine wanted him to settle. He had a grand dream: he wanted to play an important role in Europe's financial world.

He decided he should work in Scotland, the land of his birth. In about 1704, he left Venice with Katherine and made the long journey through Germany down to Holland to take a ship to Scotland. He worried about his past. In England he could still be sent to prison or even hanged, but Scotland, although it had the same king, had a different government. He could not be punished there for a crime committed in London. However, if England and Scotland joined to form a union of the two countries, as many people wanted, he would not be safe in Scotland.

Law was tired of exile. After nearly ten years travelling, he wanted to settle down; he needed a royal pardon. King William had died and Anne was now queen. Perhaps the Wilson family would accept money for their loss, and Law now had plenty of money. He began to hope that if he could show the Queen how his ideas would make money for the country, she would forgive him.

When he arrived in Edinburgh, Law was reunited with his mother, who he had not seen since he left the city as a young man. We do not know what his mother thought about his relationship with Katherine. But whatever her feelings, the family situation was peaceful and Law was able to work with new purpose.

He decided to write about his project and send a report to the Queen. In this document he suggested a bank that would print paper money based on the value of land. It was not an original idea; since the mid-seventeenth century many writers had written about it – even Daniel Defoe felt that land was the best guarantee for banks.

Law's project was clever and he wrote well, but he could not escape his past. He was a criminal and a gambler, and Queen Anne did not trust him. Although the Wilson family had agreed to his pardon, and although he begged to be allowed to work for the Queen for the rest of his life, his project was not accepted. Disappointed but still positive, Law thought his project could work in Scotland, if not in England. He was confident that his powerful friends, like the Duke of Argyll, would help him.

At the beginning of the eighteenth century, Scotland was a desperately poor country. There was little trade, money was in short supply and unemployment was high. The situation was made worse by the Darien plan. William Paterson, who had started the Bank of England, had had the idea of building a colony in Panama as a base for trade across the Atlantic and the Pacific oceans so that ships would not have to sail all the way round South America. Promising to make Scotland the richest country in the world, and claiming that the plan was risk-free, Paterson borrowed £400,000 – nearly half the money in Scotland – from optimistic investors who were eager to get rich. In 1698 five ships, with 2,000 passengers including Paterson, his wife and son, sailed from Leith. They reached Panama three months later.

The new colony was a disaster. Disease was everywhere, the Spanish attacked the colonists, the English did not help them, trade failed. When, two years later, the project ended, 1,700 of the colonists had lost their lives, including Paterson's wife and son. The individuals who had lent money were ruined, and the economic situation in Scotland was so bad that even the Bank of

Scotland, started a year after the Bank of England, was threatened.

John Law was sure he could improve the situation. He published new ideas and still today economic historians admire them because his writing and thoughts are so clear. He begins by explaining the meaning of value: 'Water is of great use' but 'of little value, because the quantity of water is much greater than the demand for it. Diamonds are of little use' but 'great value, because the demand for diamonds is much greater than the quantity of them.' He discusses the meaning of money and argues that, 'Money is not the value *for* which things are exchanged, but the value *by* which they are exchanged; the use of money is to buy goods ... money is of no other use.' This idea of money as having no value in itself but being based on something of steady value leads him to his central suggestion: for a bank with the power to print notes using land as a guarantee of value.

Law's friends thought he was right and the Duke of Argyll brought his project to the attention of the Scottish Parliament. In June 1705, the main business of the parliament was to discuss the question of union with England. After the failure of the Darien plan, many politicians felt that union would help Scotland. Besides Law's project, the parliament also looked at one from Dr Chamberlen, a man already famous in England and Scotland for his financial projects.

One parliamentary group, the Squadrone Volante, supported Law, but the national party headed by Andrew Fletcher was strongly opposed to Law's plan and supported Dr Chamberlen's. Fletcher and Law's friend, Roxburghe, became so angry that the Duke of Argyll, who was in charge of the meeting, ordered both men to their rooms to prevent a fight. Roxburghe, a polite and respectful man, obeyed, but the bad-tempered Fletcher escaped to a pub and sent a message to Roxburghe to meet him in Leith for a duel.

Roxburghe reacted and, with his friend Baillie, rushed to

Leith at six in the evening. Before the two men could pull out their swords, Baillie stopped them. The fight would not be fair, he said, because Roxburghe was injured in his right leg and could hardly stand. Fletcher had guessed that this would happen; he produced a pair of guns and offered them to Roxburghe so that he could take his choice. Baillie again stopped the fight, saying that Roxburghe could not shoot on foot. During this argument a group of law officers rode up. The two men's friends fired the guns in the air and everyone went back to Edinburgh.

This stupid quarrel did nothing to help Law, and as time went by union came ever closer. Law, not wanting to leave his homeland and still hoping for a royal pardon, wrote again to the Queen and again was refused. Exile was now the only way to avoid prison. Katherine made preparations to leave. Law spent his final days in Scotland at the gambling tables. Among his recorded successes was land worth £1,200 won from Sir Andrew Ramsay, 'one of the finest Gentlemen of his time'; after meeting John Law, Ramsay had only £100 left.

Law left Scotland and his mother. He never saw her again; she died two years later. At that time, however, such sorrow was far from his thoughts. His main aim was to find a way of putting his plans into action.

Chapter 4   The Rise of John Law

Late in 1705, Law and Katherine returned to the Continent. They lived in The Hague, waiting for the birth of their first child. Then, soon after their son, John, was born, they moved to Vienna. Law was successful at the gambling tables and won a lot of money before leaving the city. By now he had decided to concentrate on the largest European country, with the greatest population and serious economic problems – France.

Louis XIV had been king for sixty-three years. He had raised his country to commercial heights that made it the envy of Europe, and then ruined it with wars, religious quarrels and extraordinary spending. Lack of money lay at the root of all France's problems. In some years, like 1694 and 1709, the poor had no food; children lived on 'boiled grass and roots'. The King tried every known way to find money. New taxes were introduced, old taxes were increased. There were so many taxes that people feared that soon even births and marriages would be taxed. Between 1690 and 1715, coins were revalued forty times.

Law was sure that the answer was simple – the only way out was through credit. Because there was not enough gold and silver, the answer was to start a national bank and to print paper money. First, though, he had to reach and persuade the King. In 1706 Law managed a journey to Paris, but the King's Controller General did not understand Law's plans and the King himself never saw them. However, the journey was not wasted. Law met the King's nephew Philippe, Duc★ d'Orléans. Their friendship changed the course of history.

The two men shared many common interests. They were of a similar age, both were handsome, both were brilliant tennis players. Both enjoyed extraordinary success with women. But Orléans was much wilder than Law. His many lovers – actresses, servants or, more rarely, aristocrats – were chosen for their good humour, their love of food and drink and lovemaking, and their lack of interest in politics. Looks mattered little – even his own mother said, 'They do not have to be beautiful. I have often [criticized] him for choosing such ugly ones.' At night, in his Paris house, the royal palace, he sent his servants away and then gave all-night parties for his close friends. The writer, Saint-Simon, said that they made a lot of noise and when they were

★ *Duc*: the French word for *duke*.

very drunk they went to bed and began again the next day. All Paris talked about them.

But Orléans was not just another aristocratic drunk. He was a brilliant man, interested in music, literature, philosophy and science, including the science of money. He collected paintings, he played musical instruments. But he was bored because the King would not give him a powerful role.

Law spent long hours explaining his ideas to Orléans and was delighted to find someone with the intelligence and imagination to understand his plans. Encouraged by his royal friend, Law again sent his plans to the King. But despite Orléans' help and Law's great hopes, the King was cold. The problem this time was Law's religion. He was a Protestant, so the King did not trust him.

Law did not give up hope. He went to Holland and continued looking for a ruler who would listen to him. Life was hard for Katherine, but their relationship was strong. They spent long periods of time together as they travelled around Europe, and they depended on each other for friendship. In each new city Katherine's charm helped Law win powerful friends. In 1710 their second child, Kate, was born in Italy.

They returned to The Hague and filled a grand house with paintings and works of art. They became famous. Katherine happily played the role of society hostess, and they had many visitors. Law knew this would help his plans. Everyone wanted to know exactly how his fortune had been made, but Law enjoyed remaining a man of mystery.

His luck had begun to change. In 1713 France was left in ruins after years of war. Louis XIV was now seventy-five. In the last three years, his son, his grandson and his great-grandson had died. He would be followed by his second great-grandson, a child of four, and Law's friend, Orléans, would be regent.

More than ever France needed an answer to its financial problems. Law returned to Paris and wrote to the new finance minister. Orléans' support was beginning to work, and the minister wrote 'when he comes I will speak to him' at the top of Law's letter. Somehow, though, Law did not get the message and the meeting never took place, but he was confident that he would succeed. He returned to The Hague to prepare to move his family to France.

By May 1714 he was back in Paris, still trying to get an opportunity to present his projects to the King. Law's family arrived two months later and they lived, with many servants, in a large house on the place* Vendôme, then one of Paris's newest squares, where many powerful financiers lived.

In England that summer Queen Anne died. Law immediately contacted an old aristocratic Scottish friend, Stair, who had just become the British ambassador to Paris, and asked him to beg the new king, George I, to reconsider Law's position. Law was the first person Stair visited when he arrived in Paris, and Stair wrote to politicians in England saying that Law was 'the cleverest man that is' and that he had useful plans for paying the national debt. But again, Law was refused a pardon.

This made Law more committed to France, and finally he had his meeting with the finance minister, Desmarets. Law explained his plans but Desmarets was full of questions. How soon could Law begin? How would the bank work? What guarantees could Law offer? And while discussions continued, French financiers heard about Law's plans. They did not like them; they feared for their own profits but also had real worries about the project. A state bank printing paper money would never work, said Samuel Bernard, one of the wealthiest financiers, 'in a country where everything depends on the King's pleasure'. Despite the opposition, Law remained calm and optimistic. He patiently answered every one of Desmarets' questions. He could open the

* *Place*, *rue*: French words for *square* and *street*.

bank in August or even earlier. He was so sure it would work that he would use his own money as guarantee. In this grand new bank Desmarets would have an official role. Eventually Desmarets agreed; only the King still had to be persuaded.

But suddenly in August the King's health failed, and on Sunday 1 September 1715, Louis XIV, king for seventy-two years, died. Orléans acted immediately to guarantee his own position. From now until the five-year-old prince became old enough to rule, Orléans would govern France as regent. For John Law, the opportunity of which he had dreamed for so long had never seemed closer.

At the General Bank the enormous double doors on the rue St Avoye stood open. Inside, a few customers chatted before moving on to complete their deals. It was late summer 1716 and as usual business was quiet. Then a carriage arrived that was neither ordinary nor expected. The customers recognized the uniform of the servants of the Regent. The servants got out of the carriage carrying metal boxes, which they took into the bank and placed on the counter. An officer stepped forward to unlock them. Inside each box were gold and silver coins which the Regent wished to keep at the bank. The total value was millions of livres.* The other customers were amazed. They did not know that John Law and the Regent had arranged this public show to build up people's confidence in the bank and in paper money, which until now had been a joke.

The trick worked. Within days, newspapers reported that the Regent had such trust in John Law's new bank that he kept his own millions there. Newspapers which had opposed the bank changed their stories. Everyone believed that the bank would succeed because it had royal money supporting it.

But Law still had enemies, one of whom was Noailles, the new

* Livre: the name of an old French coin.

finance minister. He pretended to be friendly but really he was jealous of Law's closeness to the Regent. Noailles had found that France's financial situation was worse than anyone imagined. The national debt was over 2 billion livres with interest repayments of 90 million; tax collection was inefficient, and the income was spent three or four years before it was collected. Some advisors suggested that France should simply go bankrupt and start again. Law persuaded Orléans not to do that. He encouraged him to make the General Bank a state bank and to print paper money. Law also tried to persuade the other royal advisors. A few agreed with him, but many of Paris's most important bankers and financiers did not. Nine of thirteen members of the Regent's council voted against Law's plans. Orléans did not dare to oppose these powerful men so early in his regency. A state bank would not be created.

Law was discouraged and angry. He said that the use of banks was recognized in all commercial countries, and the Regent knew that that was true. He was afraid Law would leave France and he did not want to lose him, so he ordered Noailles to persuade Law to stay. Noailles managed to do so by promising Law that he could still be useful to the state. Law knew he had to change his ideas a little and wait. He calmed down and stayed.

If the Regent did not want a state bank then, Law thought, France should have a privately run bank, similar to the Bank of England, printing notes and financed by shareholders. Through a winter so cold that the sea froze at Calais, Law held meetings with the Regent to explain the new plans. He argued that the introduction of credit was as important as the discovery of colonies for a country; that his banking project was the quickest and safest way of building commercial confidence – it was the base for power and order in the state. When Law talked like this, money seemed a magic way to make dreams come true. Orléans was persuaded.

While Law and the Regent were holding their meetings, Noailles was trying other methods of improving the country's finances. The loans which people had made to Louis XIV to finance the wars received interest at 7 per cent, but Noailles reduced this interest to 4 per cent. He reduced short-term loans to two-thirds their previous value. He lowered salaries. He devalued coins by 50 per cent. While these methods reduced the royal debts, they caused prices to rise and people to hide their gold and silver or smuggle it abroad. The financial situation got worse; businesses went into debt, and shopkeepers closed their doors. Hundreds were bankrupted and that caused unemployment. Many turned to crime. The newspaper *Gazette de la Régence* recorded: 'The countryside is full of robbers; we dare not go out of the towns for fear of robberies which happen every night . . . nowhere is there a country like it, and if the King does not pay . . .' The whole country was sinking economically, and society itself was threatened.

Then, in 1716, Noailles tried an even more desperate method: he decided to arrest financiers and tax collectors and other speculators who he felt had profited from the problems of the country. He offered people large rewards for reporting anyone who had broken the law. Servants reported employers, wives reported husbands, lovers reported each other, children even reported parents. It was complete confusion as people tried to escape from the country. Some even killed themselves because they were so frightened of the punishments given to those who were caught.

Against this background, Law's ideas seemed to offer a painless solution. By spring he had completed his plans for a private bank, financed by himself and other shareholders, which would print notes guaranteed by gold and silver. These notes could be changed back for coins at any time. Law promised that his notes would be safe and would increase the amount of money in the economy and so help trade. His bank would offer hope and the promise of a better future.

The Regent listened. He was exhausted by other problems of state, and by his all-night parties, and tired of Noailles' unpopular methods. He wanted a quick and efficient answer, so he gave Law his complete support. He spoke to each of his advisors individually and made clear what he wanted. Almost all agreed. Saint-Simon was the only exception; he dared to speak against Law. He pointed out the two most important problems: how to stop the bank printing too much money, and how to stop the King spending too much money. These were the same problems as Bernard had noted in the time of Louis XIV: because the King was above the law, in difficult times he could misuse the bank, confidence would fail, and the holders of paper money and the economy in general would be ruined. Orléans and Law had no real answers to these points, but Saint-Simon's warnings were ignored.

Law took French nationality and in 1716 was given permission to run the General Bank for twenty years. At first people were not very interested. The bank had little money. Few trusted Law or his paper money; he was still a foreigner to them, and a gambler and, some said, a criminal. The bank struggled.

Law offered free or inexpensive banking services to attract customers. He offered foreign exchange and movement of sums of money between French cities. The Regent helped him by taking his own money to the bank. Foreigners started to use the bank, happy to have somewhere in Paris where they could change money for a reasonable price. Slowly Law began printing notes and trade began to grow. Traders liked the notes. The guarantee of being paid in coins of fixed value meant they knew exactly what something would cost or what price they would receive. In October 1716, the Regent ordered tax collectors to pay the King with Law's banknotes. A few months later, a law was passed saying that people could pay their taxes with banknotes. Eighteen months after the bank opened, there were enough profits to pay the shareholders a dividend. Law's white banknotes could be found all over France. The economic improvement which Law had promised had begun.

But the private bankers of Paris were not pleased. Law was damaging their profits. They began to plot against him and the bank. They collected together 5 million livres in banknotes and presented them for immediate payment. Law knew that public confidence was based on his promise to 'pay on demand'. And he also knew that he did not have gold and silver to the value of 5 million livres in the bank.

He told the bankers that it would take twenty-four hours to get such a large sum and he went to Noailles for help. The minister hated to admit it but he knew it was in his interest as well as Law's to save the bank. So he lent Law the coins he needed. Imagine the surprise of the bankers the next day when, expecting to find the bank in confusion, they saw the bags full of gold and silver. Law had beaten them.

However, while the bank was moving slowly towards success, Law was already looking for exciting new opportunities. One came, unexpectedly, in the form of a diamond. The enormous diamond had been smuggled out of a diamond mine in India by an employee. It was bought for £20,000 by Thomas Pitt, governor of the East India Company, who became known as Diamond Pitt. Pitt sent the diamond to London to be cut. It was almost round and perfectly white, and it was the biggest diamond that anyone had ever seen. Naturally Pitt wanted to sell it for a profit, but he soon found that in times of war and economic uncertainty people did not want such large diamonds. Louis XIV had been offered the diamond the year before he died, and even he had refused it. In 1717 Pitt came back to Paris with his diamond. Law tried to persuade the Regent to buy it. Orléans certainly wanted it, but he was frightened of what people would say. Eventually Law, with the help of Saint-Simon, did persuade him, and the Regent paid 2 million livres for it. Ever since, this great diamond has been part of the French state collection of jewels, and now it is in the Louvre museum in Paris.

But the affair of the diamond was just one of Law's many ideas. And 'the bank is not the only nor the greatest of my ideas. I will produce a work that will surprise Europe by the changes it will produce,' he wrote to the Regent. Law was looking at the riches of Africa and America, and he wanted to form an overseas trading company to explore them. The Italians, the Spanish, the Portuguese, the Dutch and the English had all made fortunes from their colonies, with their ships carrying coffee, tea, chocolate, gold, silver and many other valuable goods. It was time for France to start.

The French had an American colony, Louisiana, which stretched from the mouth of the Mississippi river north for nearly five thousand kilometres, covering what we now call Louisiana, Mississippi, Arkansas, Missouri, Illinois, Iowa, Wisconsin, Minnesota and parts of Canada. This enormous piece of land was unexplored and only Indians lived there. Most French people did not even know where it was, but many believed it was full of gold, silver and jewels.

Law said that previous overseas companies had failed because they did not have enough money and they had been badly directed. His company would have plenty of money and be well managed; it would make France the most powerful nation in the world again. Law would get the necessary money by forming a company, the Mississippi Company, and selling 200,000 shares. Anyone could share in the company's success.

Again, when the idea was discussed in parliament, many did not trust Law, some were jealous of him, and some thought he just wanted to make money for himself – he was still a foreigner. But again, the Regent supported Law. His admiration of Law had grown with the bank's profits. Law promised wealth, adventure, uncertainty, excitement, all the things Orléans enjoyed. Law was given permission to start his company, and to run it with its own army and navy for twenty-five years. As managing director of the company Law was, except in name, king of half America.

Like the bank, the company struggled at first. There was very little actual cash to pay for the ships, crews, stores, seeds, tools and all the other things needed by the colonists. Unlike the English and the Dutch, the French had not yet discovered the pleasures of share-dealing. Sales of shares were slow.

Noailles had joined with Law's enemies and was plotting against him. By January 1718, the Regent was forced to act. He invited Law and Noailles to a dinner party and asked both men to explain their plans for the future. Noailles talked about old ideas of taxes and financial controls. Law talked of having a state bank, of building up his trading company into something larger and more powerful than the world had ever seen, even of paying the national debt. Law's new ideas were much more attractive than Noailles' traditional approach. The finance minister was moved to a new job in which he would have nothing to do with Law. Noailles' place as finance minister was filled by d'Argenson. Some thought that d'Argenson knew little of finance and would take the role and its advantages while letting Law control things in secret. In fact, d'Argenson quickly made his own plans to solve the country's financial problems: he would cut government debt by devaluing the livre.

Law's main worry was for his banknotes. But as they were guaranteed for value on the day they were written, they would probably become more attractive if other forms of money were devalued. He decided to wait patiently while d'Argenson played at finance. This was a mistake.

Although the devaluation was not Law's idea, people blamed him for it. Parliament took the opportunity to attack him. Stair, the English ambassador, commented on the mood of the time; it was dangerous to employ Law because everyone was against him. 'Orléans, in the present situation of his affairs, would run a great risk in putting ... the finances into the hands of a stranger so generally hated.' Parliament boldly demanded that the Regent stop the devaluation. When he refused, parliament passed a law forbidding the payment of taxes with banknotes and forbidding all foreigners, even those who had taken French nationality, from handling royal money. The reference to Law was clear.

There was even talk that parliament was going to send officers to hang Law, but the Regent sent soldiers to guard him. It was a frightening experience for Law. At an emergency meeting called by Saint-Simon, he did not know what to do or what to say. He feared the Regent would leave him to his enemies.

But Orléans was preparing a surprise for parliament. He arranged a special meeting at which the young king would support his regent. Saint-Simon helped with the plans to defeat parliament. On 26 August, the day of the meeting, there were Swiss guards and soldiers around the royal palace, the Tuileries, Law's bank and other important buildings. The meeting began at ten in the Palace of Justice. The eight-year-old king stood on a small platform and d'Argenson made the announcement for him: 'The King chooses to be obeyed.' Parliament was defeated. Three members refused to obey and were taken to prison; the others knew their moment had passed. Once again Law, the outsider, had escaped them.

Chapter 5   Success

In spite of recent shocks, Law still had the gambler's will to win and he still wanted to get a royal pardon for the death of Wilson. He also wanted social acceptance; he had a need to belong. Like many successful businessmen today, he had political ambitions. And he had a family to look after.

By now the bank was very successful. It had 9 million livres in coins and 1.6 million in credit notes against which there was 40 million in paper money. Law carefully controlled the number of notes printed. He had learned the lesson of the Bank of Amsterdam. In December 1718 the General Bank became the Royal Bank, like a state bank today. Law rewarded the old shareholders generously, and both he himself and the Regent also profited greatly from the bank's change of ownership. Law continued to direct the bank and opened new branches in Lyon, La Rochelle, Tours, Orléans and Amiens. Because there was not much gold around, most people used his paper money for all important business deals. Law was now top banker and everyone treated him with respect.

Within five months of royal control of the bank, the writer Buvat noted in his diary that there were eight printers working night and day printing notes. These new notes could not be exchanged for their value on the day they were made but only for the value printed on them. Like coins, they could now be devalued; the principle which supported public confidence had been lost. If Law was unhappy, he gave no sign of it. He was busy reinvesting profits from his bank shares in property. He bought land from the Princess of Condé for 100,000 livres and a palace, the Hôtel de Soissons, from the Prince of Carignan for 750,000. The Hôtel became the home of the Mississippi Company, but the clever prince did not sell Law the beautiful gardens and later made a profit by letting them as a marketplace for share-dealing.

At around this time, John Law's brother William joined him in Paris. William had trained in Edinburgh as a goldsmith and was, Law believed, one of his most trusted friends. William had been a director of the General Bank and had worked for some time for Law in London. Among William's friends was George

Middleton, a top London banker, who the Laws had used to make investments in diamonds, Scottish land, and shares in the English South Sea and East India Companies. Before coming to Paris, William had married Rebecca Dives, a beautiful, rich young woman. Law and Katherine helped the newly married couple find a large house, servants and several carriages, and introduced them into society.

Law was anxious to encourage local industry, which he believed was necessary for national wealth. He brought about 900 skilled workers, like clock and watch-makers and metal-workers, from England to France. They lived on land belonging to the Regent's daughter and received high salaries. There would be great demand for the goods they made in the economic boom. They had made a good move.

Law's main concern, however, was the price of the Mississippi Company's shares, still disappointingly low. He decided that he had to take control of French trade and state finances. This was a bold idea, the same idea as he had used as a young gambler, in fact, to increase his chances of winning by controlling the situation as much as possible. First he obtained some overseas trade – the right to tobacco-farming in the colonies. Tobacco-smoking was just beginning to become popular and the profit from this right, as many investors quickly realized, could only grow.

The French East India and China Company had been badly managed and was making losses. Law suggested it should become part of the Mississippi Company. Such a worldwide company would be very risky, but Law made it seem possible. More shares would be sold, this time for cash only, to finance the building of two dozen large ships to increase French overseas trade.

As usual d'Argenson opposed Law; even the Regent was anxious about the plan. Realizing the doubters would only be silenced if he could show that the plan was completely safe, Law and several important friends and investors agreed that the shares could be paid for over ten months. The money to build the ships would not be needed all at once. Law found five people willing to invest a million livres each; he himself invested 2.5 million. This show of confidence persuaded the Regent, and on Sunday 23 May 1719 he gave permission for Law to run the combined companies.

Beneath the confidence, even Law himself worried about the plan. 'On Monday night I did not sleep; I had gained a great confidence with the public and I feared losing it by the action I had taken,' he later admitted. In fact, he had won his gamble. Everyone believed that Law was sure of success and the cleverest of them began to invest. Then the others followed. The price of shares rose rapidly, and 50 million paper notes were printed so that people could buy the shares due out at the end of the month. Then Law showed his understanding of psychology, that demand is increased by reducing supply. To buy one new share, an investor had to own four old ones. The old shares were called mothers and the new shares were daughters. So, in the summer of 1719, the early investors saw the value of their investment rise as France enjoyed its first share boom. Law promised to pay shareholders a 12 per cent dividend in the following year. As the bank printed more notes and gave people loans to buy and deal in shares, prices continued to rise. Then Law bought the right to make coins, and paid for this with more shares – granddaughters. To buy one granddaughter, you had to own four mothers and one daughter.

Outside the Mississippi Company office, all through the summer, Parisians went mad. Shares which had been sold for 490 livres three months before now cost 3,500. There was a party atmosphere. On the evening before St Louis' Day, 25 August, thousands of people went to the Jardin des Tuileries to enjoy music and celebrations. At the end of the evening they found their way out blocked because an official had forgotten to open one of the gates. Impatience became panic as thieves stole gold and silver objects, watches, diamond crosses, handkerchiefs and even pieces of people's clothes. In the panic eleven women fell and were killed. Hundreds more suffered broken arms and legs, and shock.

News of the disaster reached the rest of Europe at the same time as Law's next daring idea. He offered to be responsible for the national debt of 1.2 billion livres at 3 per cent interest and to pay 52 million for the right to collect taxes. At the time this right was rented by the government to a group of forty private financiers called the Farmers General. This group was led by four men, the Pâris brothers. They collected indirect taxes like taxes on salt and alcohol, and made large profits for themselves. They were dishonest and inefficient. Law saw injustice in the advantages that this system gave to the Farmers General. He wanted to get rid of them, not realizing how violently they would react. Law financed his latest plans by selling four more groups of shares. Anyone could buy these – you did not need to own shares already – so anyone could grow rich by buying into the Mississippi dream.

These new shares were sold at the Mississippi Company's new offices in Paris's old commercial centre, the rue Quincampoix, a street that today lies near the Pompidou Centre in the Les Halles district. The rue Quincampoix is a long, narrow street which for years had been a centre for money-changers and businessmen raising capital for new adventures. In lively markets, news is an important tool that helps traders see where prices might move next. Today's traders have news services like Reuters and Bloomberg who can supply up-to-date information and prices. In the eighteenth century, there was talk. News of the colonies, government actions and Law's future plans were discussed endlessly in the rue Quincampoix. So many people came that the surrounding streets were blocked by horses and carriages.

D'Argenson, the finance minister, who lived in rue Quincampoix, was angry when one day in November he spent more than an hour caught in a traffic jam. Eventually carriages were forbidden, gates were put up to control the crowds, and guards stopped night dealings which kept the neighbours awake. In a useless attempt to keep order, one entrance was made for rich and aristocratic investors, and another for everyone else.

In the mornings a bell rang, the gates opened and politeness was lost. Aristocrats pushed against their servants; priests competed with singers and actresses; judges did business with thieves; Italians, Dutch and English mixed with the French. Daniel Defoe described the extraordinary scenes: 'the inconvenience of the darkest and nastiest street in Paris does not stop the crowds of people . . . coming to buy and sell . . . in the open place; where . . . they go up to the ankles in dirt, every step they take.' Even the nine-year-old king felt the atmosphere. When he saw a plan of Paris, he demanded that rue Quincampoix should be coloured in gold.

Paris high society was surprised by the number of poor people who made money through Mississippi Company shares. Money was easy to borrow and because you only needed to put down 10 per cent of a share price to start, people rushed to sell their palaces, their diamonds, their cows and their crops to join in. The aristocrats were worried. And even the writer Voltaire was puzzled. He wrote to a friend, 'It is good to come to the country . . . Have you really all gone mad in Paris? I only hear talk of millions.' He had heard that everyone who was rich before was now poor, and people who had been poor were now rich. He wondered if this was reality. Had half the nation found magic in the printed paper money? Was Law a god, or a criminal who was poisoning himself with a drug he was giving to everyone?

There were dozens of stories of 'Mississippians' who were poor one day and rich the next. There was the story of a servant who made so much money that he bought himself a carriage, but when it was delivered, he forgot that he should ride in it and went to stand at his old place behind it. Or the story of the Widow Chaumont, who came to Paris just to collect a debt. She invested in the Mississippi shares and quickly made millions. She bought a palace and every week held famous dinner parties where guests ate a cow, six sheep and several chickens. Law's own carriage driver made so much money that he left his job, employed two drivers, offered Law first choice and took the other driver for himself.

By October the share price had reached 6,500 livres. The traders on rue Quincampoix operated independently; prices at one end of the street could be quite different from prices at the other. Fortunes made in one hour could be lost in the next. Property was also bought and sold. Houses on rue Quincampoix were bought or rented by clever businessmen. A small property previously rented for 800 livres a year could be divided into twenty or thirty small offices and rented for 400 livres each a month. Huts were put up in side streets or on rooftops and rented out for large amounts. As the crowds continued to grow, bars, cake shops and restaurants charged very high prices for their services. All normal sense of value was lost. A window into this world is opened in the paintings of Watteau, in which colourful figures in beautiful clothes go on picnics or shop for works of art. Money, Defoe said, moved as quickly as the waters of the River Seine. People were buying gold and silver objects, clothes, carpets, and furniture made from wood brought back in the Mississippi Company ships. The Regent's mother noted that it was unbelievable what wealth there was in France at that time: 'Everybody speaks in millions. I don't understand it at all.'

John Law was now an international star. Princes and priests rushed to meet him; aristocratic ladies came too. Women had always liked him, but now he was rich and powerful so they admired him more than ever. Madame de Bouchu was one bold lady Law was eager to avoid. She followed him to a dinner given by an aristocratic rival although she had not been invited. She ordered her servant to drive in front of the house and shout 'Fire'. All the guests ran into the street. Madame de Bouchu saw Law and tried to kidnap him, but he managed to escape. Law remained generally humorous and polite, but as a very private person he found it all hard to bear.

However, Paris talk said Law did take lovers – perhaps Claudine de Tencin, who had been a favourite of the Regent and of the foreign minister Dubois; perhaps Mademoiselle de Nail, the favourite of Prince Soubise; perhaps, some said, the Regent's mother, although she was sixty-eight. Probably these stories were not true, but Katherine was hurt although later events showed that her affection for Law remained and she continued in her role of society wife. Law's children too moved in high society circles. His son, John, learned to hunt and to dance with the young Louis XV. His daughter, Kate, received offers of marriage from aristocrats but Law turned them all down; he was a protective father. Law himself received public honours, and as he passed through the streets people shouted, 'God save the King and Monsieur Law!' Honours came from abroad too; Edinburgh gave him the freedom of the city.

At first, all this attention did not change Law. He lived quite simply and continued to invest in property and art. Perhaps Katherine and the children kept his feet firmly on the ground. He still enjoyed an evening with friends playing a few games of cards. When an old aristocratic friend, Ilay, visited Law's house, he found the great man writing to the gardener at Lauriston about the plants he wanted in the garden.

As the economy grew, Law worked hard on improvements. He started a programme of public building of bridges and roads. Money was given to the university and the Scots College where his father was buried. He started to make the tax system simpler and to get rid of unnecessary officials – inspectors for cloth, for wood, for paper, for meat and fish; there had even been an inspector for pigs' tongues. Law introduced a new national tax system based on income. These changes made the officials, the financiers and the members of parliament very angry, but they delighted the public. 'The people went dancing and jumping about the streets,' wrote Defoe; 'they now pay [no tax] for wood, coal . . . oil, wine, beer, bread, cards, soap, cattle, fish.'

There were so many newly rich people that the word 'millionaire' was invented to describe them. Perhaps as many as 500,000 foreigners from Venice, Genoa, Geneva, England, Holland and Spain came to Paris to deal in shares, as well as people from all over France. Public transport was fully booked for months; every hotel room in the city was full. Journalists loved the get-rich-quick atmosphere, but many high society Parisians hated the foreigners and criticized Law for selling them shares. Law welcomed the foreigners because they brought with them the gold and silver which the paper money system needed as its base. And by now an enormous quantity of notes had been printed; economists think perhaps as many as 1.2 billion by the end of 1719. There were also 624,000 shares sold, worth about 4.8 billion livres; the King and the Mississippi Company owned about a third of these. Thanks to Law's magic system, France was richer by about 5.2 billion livres and the Regent and his family had also earned fortunes. And still, into the winter of 1719, share prices rose.

Two years earlier, King George I had pardoned Law, but Law gave the pardon to the Regent to prove his loyalty to France. Now stories started about Law's political views. His old friend Stair, the British ambassador in Paris, now opposed him, claiming that Law was against the British and threatening the British economy. He wrote to England that Law wanted to make France 'much higher than she ever was before and put her in a condition to give the law to all Europe; that he can ruin the trade and credit of England and Holland whenever he pleases; that he can break our bank'. Stair also reported that the Regent was angry with Law because of his pride and ambition, because Law wanted to be absolute master. Other reports do not support this picture, but the English were very worried about France's growing power. They also feared that the tourists who were investing in the Mississippi Company were emptying England of her coins. But they could do nothing. Law was too powerful to attack, and the next year Stair was called back to England.

Now Law wanted more recognition for what he had done for France; he wanted a position within the government. His religion was a problem. Oddly for the grandchild of a minister of the Church of Scotland, religion was not important to Law. He joined the Church of Rome and made his children change too; Katherine was 'very much upset about it,' said the Regent's mother, but Law ignored her feelings. The ceremony of Law's acceptance into the Church of Rome took place in December 1719, and the priest later received 200,000 livres worth of shares. Law began giving money generously to churches and to good causes. On 5 January 1720, he got what he wanted: he was made Controller General of Finance. Few people were surprised.

Chapter 6   Mississippi Madness

Ever since Law had taken control of the Louisiana colony, wonderful reports of it had appeared in France's official newspaper, the *Nouveau Mercure*. Journalists described it as a rich land in which the climate was gentle, the earth productive, the woods full of trees suited for building and for trading, the countryside full of wild horses and cattle. In this wonderful land, a story in September 1717 said, the ground was rich with gold and silver and other, important metals – only people to work were lacking. These optimistic stories continued for three more years.

The city of New Orleans was built in 1718 at the mouth of the Mississippi to control the trade on the Mississippi–Missouri rivers. By 1719 stories claimed that it was a crowded city of 800 very comfortable houses, each one with land for the support of the families. It was all a dream. The colony was struggling to stay alive. Between 1717 and 1720, of the thousands who made the hard journey to Louisiana, over half died on the way or returned exhausted and disappointed with what they had found. Hundreds more died of disease or hunger. No gold, silver or jewels had been found and de Bienville, the colony's governor, reported to the company in 1719 that New Orleans had four small houses and the colonists lived only by trading with the natives.

All the exciting stories had been invented by Law, more as a trick to build confidence than as real lies. He was sure that with enough time and money the colony would be the success that everyone believed it already was. Confidence in all the shares and all the paper money depended on public belief that the colony was rich and was sure to become richer. Law had no choice. He had to keep the facts secret.

There was another problem – there were too few willing colonists. Law offered rewards to encourage people to become colonists. He would pay them from the time they reached Louisiana until they were settled; they would be given land, animals and flour. But even Law could not persuade the French to leave France for an unknown and undeveloped colony.

He tried leading by example. In partnership with an Irishman, Richard Cantillon, and the English financier John Gage, Law bought land near the Ouachita river to the west of the Mississippi, in what is now the state of Arkansas. While Law and his partners observed from their comfortable Paris houses, around a hundred settlers, including carpenters, mine-workers and gardeners were employed to go and search for metals and grow tobacco. The group, under Cantillon's brother Bernard, left La Rochelle on the slave ship *St Louis* in March 1719. Three months later, they arrived in Louisiana. As Law had hoped, other partnerships followed his example – some aristocrats, some shareholders, including the famous Widow Chaumont, and several of his English, Irish and Scottish friends. As soon as he knew his group had arrived safely, Law talked about its success. Society heard that pure silver of a high quality had been discovered on his land. Few suspected that these whispers came from Law's imagination, not from news from the settlers.

Bernard Cantillon and his team found themselves in a terrible place where the struggle to live prevented any attempts to farm or to mine. The colonists suffered from diseases and fevers. They were in danger of attack by Indians, who needed constant payments to remain friendly. In March 1719 1,500 French colonists were killed in one attack, but this, too, was kept secret. There was also danger from the Spanish settlements to the west and the English settlement to the east; Louisiana was sandwiched between them. Cantillon and his group, like others before them, did not realize how bad things were until they arrived, and then it was too late to go back. Within four years disease and other dangers had reduced the group's size to a quarter of its original number. There were no quick profits for Law and his partners. Another two centuries would pass before the true wealth beneath the ground was found – not in silver, gold or jewels, but in oil.

Law moved to speed things up. The problems, as he saw them, were the lack of settlers and the lack of support systems. He reacted first with orders for many new ships, eight or nine from England and another four from France, which would take the company to about thirty ships, more even than the rival English East India Company. He also had a plan to find settlers. New laws were passed, and every criminal, beggar and servant unemployed for more than four days could be listed and sent to the colony. An army of commercial soldiers was employed by the Mississippi Company to catch people and take them to the ships. In Paris Law was allowed to take orphans and young people from poor-houses. About 4,000 people, among them the most defenceless and the most dangerous citizens, were sent to the colony to increase the number of settlers and to provide the necessary, unskilled workers. The first group of women received the warmest welcome from the male settlers, and the women quickly found husbands. Problems came when two men claimed the last woman and the matter had to be decided by a fight.

At first, few opposed the transportations. Saint–Simon said that if they had been done with wisdom and care, they would have succeeded and Paris and the country would have been freed of some useless and dangerous people. But the commercial soldiers were cruel and violent and soon everyone hated them. If they could not find enough listed people they took anyone they could find, because they were paid for each 'settler' they caught. In addition, private individuals paid the soldiers to get rid of their enemies; an unwanted relative, difficult son, inconvenient competitor, demanding husband or wife could be sent to Louisiana. Sometimes the soldiers even kidnapped children. The people taken were cruelly treated and shut up without food or water.

Law, conscious of these problems, tried to encourage willing settlers, especially young married couples. On visits to the Paris poor-houses, he offered rewards to couples who would marry and go to the colony. In September 1719 the wedding took place of eighty young girls and eighty specially pardoned criminals. While the marriage was taking place, the couples were held together by heavy iron chains. Afterwards, guarded by a company of soldiers, they walked, still in chains, through the streets of Paris before being sent to La Rochelle for transportation. The chains upset the public and soon after that a similar wedding took place in which the couples were joined by flowers.

Even the promise of freedom could not overcome the criminals' fear of transportation. Fights started at the ports. On 20 January 1720, it was reported that nineteen married couples in prison waiting for departure attacked their guard, took his keys and set themselves free. At La Rochelle 150 girls jumped on their guards and attacked them with their nails and teeth. The fight was only stopped when the soldiers shot at the girls, killing twelve and using their guns to force the others on to the ship. By early 1720 there were so few French settlers that Law had to invite large numbers of foreigners. Although Irish, Scottish, Swiss, German and other non-French settlers were easier to encourage, the soldiers continued their terrible work. Some attempt was made to control them: they had to work in groups, not as individuals, and they were given uniforms. But their cruelty, for which the public blamed Law, continued.

No one understood why Law seemed to ignore public opinion about the soldiers. It was not because he himself was cruel but because he was worried about more urgent matters. Weeks after becoming Controller General, he faced the most difficult situation of his career. Share prices were still rising out of control and his enemies – the financiers, the tax inspectors and the councillors of the parliament, whose incomes he had reduced – had joined together again. His whole system was in danger, so Law was understandably slow to react to public pressure about the soldiers. Slowly the message did reach him and the transportations were stopped in May 1720.

By then, though, Paris and the wider world had realized the dangers of paper money and the struggle that lay in front of Law. To save the bank, the Mississippi Company and the fortunes of thousands of investors, Law created a financial storm.

Chapter 7   Dark Days

On 30 December 1719, Law entered the office of the Mississippi Company and spoke at the annual general meeting. A sense of expectation could be felt. Within the past few months, the share prices had dropped from a high of over 10,000 livres to 7,500, and then gone up to 9,400. Even among this informed circle of directors, few understood why. Was the company doing well? If so, why had the price fallen? If not, how long would the recovery last? Law appeared to have no worries. With his usual charm and confidence, he said the company was doing well. Overseas trade was increasing and things looked so good that he would pay shareholders a dividend of 200 livres. This was the very best kind of good news.

We do not know if anyone at the meeting had enough direct contact with the colony to have any idea of the true situation there. We do not know if any of them suspected that Law had fixed the dividend, not in relation to company profits, but to support public confidence in the share price. But behind closed doors, other, cleverer investors were beginning to question the Mississippi Company and its shares. News from Louisiana was starting to come through.

The climbing share price had been fed by the enormous sums of paper notes now in the economy. Law knew this could not continue: the bank did not have enough gold and silver as a base. The system would be destroyed if people began to doubt it. Confidence was everything – but confidence was increasingly weak.

In the side streets and offices of the rue Quincampoix, business continued as usual. Dealers, taking advantage of the free market, became greedier and more dishonest. A new trade began – a buyer could pay a small amount now for a share to be delivered for an agreed price at an agreed time in the future. Investors believed that when they got their shares, they would be worth even more than the price they had agreed to pay for them. Law saw this as a particular problem. He himself had caused the great drop and then rise in share prices in December 1719. First he had tried to stop share prices rising higher by refusing to lend people money from the bank. Then, when he had seen how fast the prices fell, he panicked and started lending again.

To stop the dishonesty in the rue Quincampoix, company offices were opened in the new year to buy and sell shares at fixed prices. Law found himself forced to pay out large sums to buy unwanted shares.

Law had another serious problem; silver and gold were leaving the bank as many investors, believing that the boom was ending, exchanged their paper money for coins. One of the first to leave was Law's friend, the Irish banker Cantillon, possibly the only person who understood how dangerous Law's actions were. Cantillon knew a good deal – in money, shares, wine or art – and he did not let personal loyalty stand in the way of profit. Perhaps he had the advantage of inside information gathered over several bottles of wine shared with Law. He was one of the few people who saw that shares would rise again after their drop, and he made a profit of over £50,000 in a few weeks. He also had information from his brother in Louisiana; he knew it was time to get out. He took his winnings and left Paris for a tour of Italy to enjoy the sights and invest in art.

Cantillon was the first to turn his back on Law, but he was not alone. Several other important shareholders followed his example, and by December they had become so many that the bank was seriously threatened. Most investors sold shares for banknotes and then exchanged the banknotes for coins and either hid them or sent them abroad. The most famous seller was the Prince de Conti. Angry with Law, he took 4.5 million livres to the bank and demanded coins. Law had to agree and Conti needed three carriages to carry away the coins.

By the end of 1720, 500 million livres in silver and gold had been taken out of the country and more was on its way. Sellers of goods did not want to take paper money. In February, cattle sellers bringing their animals to the market at Poissy refused to accept anything except gold and silver. Their customers, the butchers of Paris, were forced to hire a carriage to return to the city and collect the coins.

Many investors, including the clever Widow Chaumont, bought property, and within a few months the price of land increased by three or four times. All prices were rising. The recently arrived British official Daniel Pulteney had difficulty living on his salary and had to ask for an increase. Prices of basic goods like bread were also rising, causing problems for the poor, and they were rising quickly – 25 per cent between December and January.

Law had always thought that markets should be allowed to develop freely and that control was against the principles on which credit must be built. Now he changed his mind. He decided that power, which had created the system, could be used to support it. Turning to legal methods, he acted rapidly and forcefully.

On 28 January, just three weeks after he had become Controller General, he passed a law to stop coins being sent abroad or hidden. But again his theory was mistaken. Faced with unpopular laws, people will always look for an escape route. The cleverest turned to diamonds and other jewels, which they quickly sent abroad. Others, more daringly, smuggled money over the border. Law reacted more strongly than anyone expected. On 4 February, the buying and wearing of diamonds and other jewels were forbidden. So instead investors turned to silver and gold; dishes, bowls, plates, even furniture made of the metals were bought at enormously inflated prices. Two weeks later, this escape route was also closed: a new law forbade the production and sale of all gold and silver objects except religious ones. Within days the price of crosses rose sharply.

The high share price and the over-supply of money were next for Law's cuts. He called a special meeting of shareholders. About 200 of the richest Mississippi millionaires attended, dressed in much finer clothes than the Regent, the Duc de Bourbon and the Prince de Conti, who were also there. Law announced that the Mississippi Company would control the bank. This appeared to be a small change because he was already the director of both, but it allowed him to make another important change. The 100,000 shares held by the state would be bought back by the company for 300 million livres, plus an additional monthly payment for the next ten years. Law argued that this would help the company and control the money supply. However, some people thought that while Law was trying to stop other investors leaving, he was actually encouraging the King to do so. After buying the state's shares, Law closed down the company sales offices and stopped official support of the share price.

This was bad news for the investors. Within a week, shares dropped 26 per cent from around 9,500 to 7,800 livres. The public was shocked. 'The anger of the people is so violent and so universal against Law that I think ... that in ... one month, he will be pulled to pieces,' wrote Stair happily.

Caught between public anger and the falling supply of coins, Law had to take even stronger action. On 27 February, he passed a law that forbade the possession of more than 500 livres worth of silver or gold and forced all future payments of more than 100 livres to be made in banknotes. All extra gold had to be brought to the bank and exchanged for paper. Anyone who did not obey was punished, and spies were encouraged by promises of large rewards. Any house – a palace or a hut – could be searched. It was like the worst methods of Noailles again. Servants spied on their employers, children spied on their parents. People were so frightened of punishment that the crowds who took their silver and gold to the bank felt safer when they returned with paper.

At the royal palace the Regent was anxiously watching the situation develop. As always, he was looking for an easy way out. He feared that Law's unpopularity would affect his own position. And as Law felt that the Regent doubted him, his own confidence fell. Law's enemies told terrible stories about him. Stair claimed that the Regent had threatened to have Law imprisoned in the Bastille. It seems certain that the worry over losing the Regent's support, on which Law's position and his family's future depended, had a very negative effect on Law. His confidence failed, and the reports of servants, enemies and friends suggest that he was extremely anxious. He could not sleep and suffered attacks of nerves. He had sudden angry tempers and was unreasonable even with his close family. 'He gets out of bed almost every night, and runs, mad, about the room making a terrible noise, sometimes singing and dancing, at other times swearing, staring and stamping, quite out of himself,' said Stair, who had heard this from one of Law's servants. The usually calm Katherine was alarmed.

A fortnight after removing support for the shares, Law changed the decision. He announced that the share-sales offices would reopen, and he fixed the share price at 9,000 livres. His enemies were pleased because in reality these actions made an already terrible situation worse. Crowds frightened by the sudden changes and worried about the financial position rushed to the Bank to cash in their shares, and the printers printed more money to pay for them. Law took the most serious decision of his career. If the balance between paper and coins could not be saved, he decided that he had to get rid of gold and silver completely. While paper money would remain unchanged, coins made from metal would be devalued against the livre. Within two months for gold, and nine months for silver, they would stop being used as money inside France. France would depend completely on paper.

It was a step too far. In a country noted for its financial traditionalism, a money system based on anything except gold and silver could not be imagined. Law was suspected of changing the base on which society was built and which it needed for its continuation. Even the Regent's mother, who until now had admired Law, was against the change: 'For forty-eight years now I have never been without some beautiful gold pieces in my pocket . . . Monsieur Law is certainly terribly hated.'

Opinion was divided then, and still is, over what Law was trying to achieve. Some, like Daniel Pulteney, believed he was reducing the value of gold and silver to collect it into the bank, and that he would use the gold to buy Europe's silver and bring it back to France. Law's enemies thought he was building up supplies of silver for his own use rather than for the national good. Later writers saw these changes as the actions of a drowning man.

The financial storm had a further bad effect for which Law was held responsible. Paris suffered a crime wave. There was a plague of kidnappings, violent robberies and murders, for which the envy, uncertainty, big wins and big losses which Law had caused were blamed. In one particularly horrible crime, the body of a woman cut into small pieces was found inside an overturned carriage. It was said that she had been murdered after being robbed of 300,000 livres in banknotes.

Europe was particularly shocked by the story of a young aristocrat, Antoine Joseph de Horn. Greedy for money to gamble on shares, de Horn with two others, de Mille and d'Étampes, planned to rob a rich shareholder called Lacroix, who was known to carry quantities of shares and large sums of money about with him. On the excuse of buying his shares, de Horn agreed to meet Lacroix in a bar on the corner of the rue Quincampoix.

D'Étampes waited outside while the others took Lacroix into a back room, threw a tablecloth over his head and knifed him several times in the chest. But, hearing his cries, one of the bar staff realized what was happening and locked the attackers in the room. However, the attackers jumped from a window and escaped. D'Étampes ran to the street where the horses were waiting and got away. De Mille headed for the crowds in the rue Quincampoix but was quickly caught. De Horn, who had twisted his ankle while trying to escape, pretended that he himself had been attacked, but when de Mille was brought to the bar, de Horn was recognized and caught. The next day both men had their trial and were found guilty – their punishment was to be killed by being broken on the wheel.

This was a particularly horrible punishment, usually kept for poor criminals. Prisoners were tied to a wooden wheel and had all their bones broken with iron tools – first their arms, then their legs, and finally their chest. De Horn's family, upset at the thought of their relative dying such a death, begged the Regent to spare him. Unusually, the Regent remained firm and, according to several reports, replied with the words of the great French writer Corneille, '*Le crime fait la honte, et non pas l'échafaud.*' ('The crime is the dishonour, not the punishment.') Four days after the murder, on 26 March 1720, a crowd gathered to watch de Horn and his friend being killed. De Horn took three-quarters of an hour to die.

Law tried to take advantage of the crime wave. He had always hated the dishonesty of the rue Quincampoix and now he had a reason to close the place down. Crowds were forbidden to meet in the rue Quincampoix and to deal in shares anywhere except through the official company offices.

More and more paper money was still being printed. By May 1720 there were 2.6 billion livres in banknotes, double the amount in January. The country was full of paper. Fearing that his system would crash, Law made his most desperate and probably worst change. On 21 May, a holiday weekend when most of his enemies were conveniently out of town, he announced that shares then priced at 9,000 livres would, by December, be worth only 5,000. The value of banknotes would also be reduced until they were worth 50 per cent of their present value. These changes, he argued, were for the national good, to re-balance paper and the supply of coins on which France depended for foreign trade. Nobody would suffer. The same share dividend would be paid, and the balance between paper notes and silver would return to what it had been before the devaluations announced in March.

No one believed him. In the last five months, coins had been devalued and people had been forbidden to wear jewellery. Law had left them only with paper. But through all the changes, through every twist and turn of financial plans, he had promised that the value of the paper money would not change. He had broken this promise and now, to the public, he had shown himself to be a liar and a cheat. Everyone felt they were going to be robbed of half of what they had.

The day after the announcement, an angry crowd went to the bank. When they found it closed, they began to throw stones at it. For three days there was trouble on the streets of Paris. Crowds gathered each day outside the bank, throwing stones and shouting, while inside officials struggled to deal with the crowds of investors exchanging banknotes at the new value.

The widespread hatred of John Law was dangerous for his family too. On a trip with her daughter and just two servants for protection, Katherine was attacked by a threatening crowd and was forced to find safety in a friend's house. Law can only have been made more unhappy as he realized how he had put his family in danger. The children now spent most of their time in the country homes of their father's friends. Katherine, who was increasingly worried about Law's mental state, bravely remained in Paris.

At the royal palace, the Regent tried to remain calm and wait for the storm to pass. He had failed to realize the anger which the law of 21 May would cause, and now he was sorry that he had agreed to it. Law's enemies took the chance to act. On the following Monday, an emergency meeting of parliament was called. Claiming that Law and the other directors of the bank were dishonest and bankrupt, and should be punished by death, parliament demanded that the new law be changed. Orléans had never felt so frightened. Worried that his regency might be ended, he privately admitted that he wished he had never become involved in any of John Law's projects. Law was called to the royal palace to explain himself. He faced the members calmly while both his old friend, the Duc de Bourbon, and his old enemy, d'Argenson, attacked him. The battle was lost. Knowing that if he remained in office, parliament would attack him further, Law offered to give up his job. The Regent did not agree. A week later, however, giving in to Law's enemies, Orléans changed the law reducing the value of paper money and shares and both were put back to their former values. Law knew that these changes would destroy public confidence even further. A few days later, all the earlier limits on owning silver and gold were lifted. But, as one joker said, 'The permission comes when nobody has any left.'

Frightened by all the changes, investors rushed to sell Mississippi shares and put their money somewhere safer, even if they suffered very heavy losses. Prices dropped to 4,000 livres in one week. Defoe reported that country people were leaving Paris as quickly as they had rushed there in the past.

France's ruin was England's gain. Many disappointed Mississippi shareholders chose to reinvest in English South Sea shares. The previous month, watching developments in France carefully, the South Sea Company managed to beat its rival, the Bank of England, and win a second deal with the government for another £30 million of national debt and the sale of more shares. A crowd of English and foreign investors was now rushing to London, as they had rushed, less than a year earlier, to Paris. The sudden increase of new money created a flood of companies to take advantage of the new fashion for financial gambling. People did not know what many of these companies were for, but they still invested in them.

In Paris the atmosphere was tense. By the end of the month, the Regent's Secretary of State informed Law that the Regent had decided to sack him from his position as France's Controller General. Law was ordered not to leave his house. Sixteen Swiss Guards remained outside his place Vendôme home for his own protection. That is what the Secretary of State said. It was clear, however, that Law was in prison in his own house. Law seemed to remain calm, but privately he had a real fear that his enemies' next act would be to demand his death – and that if they did, the Regent would not prevent it.

Chapter 8   Plague

Law used his old gambling tricks – hiding his feelings and following a plan. The morning after losing his position, with the guards outside his door and officials investigating his private papers at the bank, he asked for an urgent meeting with the Regent. The reply was rapid: the Duc de la Force was sent to take Law to the royal palace, where he left him to wait. Eventually, after several hours, a messenger informed Law that the Regent was unable to see him. Law returned to his house, knowing that the insult was intended – and that his enemies were delighted.

But, despite appearances, the Regent had not forgotten him. The public troubles had allowed Law's enemies – particularly d'Argenson and the Pâris brothers – to pressure the Regent into giving up on Law and his system. Orléans had only three years of regency left before Louis XV would be old enough to rule, and parliament was whispering that it might try to get rid of him even sooner. Fearing for himself, the Regent had decided to pretend to agree with the members of parliament, and then to try to trap them. Although Law failed to realize it, the Regent's actions were part of a plan. He had invested too much in Law's ideas to give them up without a fight. The Regent would only give Law up if he had to.

For Law, hope and an idea of the Regent's plans came when, late that night, he was secretly called to the royal palace. There the Regent greeted him warmly and listened carefully to his many ideas for solving the problems of the bank and the company. The next day, the guards at Law's house were removed and Law's friends felt brave enough to tell the world that he was the only man who could get them all out of their difficulties. Law worked continuously for the next forty-eight hours, returning to his original idea of supporting credit but keeping it under firm control. At a council meeting two days later, to everyone's surprise, Law entered as if the events of the past days had never happened. His system, he announced, was ready.

Law's enemies were shocked. Somehow he had got free and, the Regent informed them, would return to an important official job and as managing director of the bank and the Mississippi Company.

But although he was the royal favourite, this did not mean that Law's worries were over. Loyalties changed quickly in political life. Bourbon, Conti and de la Force, knowing how much they had gained, fearful of how much they could lose, usually supported him, but their support depended on their understanding of the political situation. No one wanted to be close to a failure and to put their own situation at risk. Law's return was bad news for his enemies. D'Argenson was sacked from his job and sent into retirement. The Pâris brothers were sent to the countryside. But the changes to Law's advantage were limited: parliament still opposed him and most of his enemies in the council remained in their posts.

At the grand offices of the bank the investigation into the accounts was coming to an end. Everyone believed it would support the Regent's friendship with Law. And, in fact, a week later the investigators' report said that they had found no irregularities. Law's enemies were later proved correct; the investigation had found that a large number of notes had been printed without permission, but to save the Regent embarrassment this had been kept secret.

◆

In other European countries the speculative boom was still building up. By the summer of 1720 the English financial boom was dangerously high. Shares that had traded for £130 in January were selling for £1,050 at the end of June. As in France, every level of society – ministers, poor widows, kings, princes, soldiers, farmers, famous scientists, philosophers, writers, artists – caught the disease, borrowed money and joined the crowd of investors, though few people fully understood the complications. Even the great scientist Isaac Newton took part; when asked for advice on the subject, he replied that he could calculate the movements of the heavenly bodies but he could not do the same for the madness of people. 'South Sea fever increases every day,' wrote Daniel Defoe in early August. 'The city ladies buy South Sea jewels, hire South Sea servants, and take new country South Sea houses; the gentlemen have South Sea carriages, and buy South Sea land.' The boom in London's other companies continued equally wildly. People were running from one coffee-house to another and from one pub to another, to buy shares without examining what the projects were. The general cry was, 'Let us buy something, we don't care what it is,' reported a London newspaper on 11 June 1720.

On the Continent, too, people rushed to make effortless fortunes. By the middle of the summer, Dutch West Indies shares had doubled in price since the beginning of the year; Dutch East India shares were similarly popular and rose from £800 to £1,000.

In Paris the story was very different. Law returned to the bank's offices in July to find crowds gathered outside in the summer heat in the hope of exchanging their banknotes for coins. It was, and still is, every banker's worst fear: confidence disappears and everyone wants to take their money out of the bank at the same time. Law had always been a man of high principles. The desire to do good, to bring happiness and wealth was, he always claimed, much more important to him than the desire for personal wealth or position. Now, seeing people's suffering, he was more deeply hurt than by any criticisms from his equals. He *had* to find an answer.

Only about 2 per cent of the money now in circulation was in silver and gold. To make this stretch as far as possible, and to make sure the poorest had some coins, he decided on a system of control. From early June, only a single 10-livre note per person could be exchanged, and the bank opened twice a week to change 100-livre paper into smaller notes. Financial balance could return, he decided, if the number of shares and banknotes was reduced, and the value of coins increased. Busy with this, Law failed to notice that his enemies were quietly waiting for a chance to act against him. When enough paper had been removed and the system was weakened, they would step in.

The removal of banknotes and shares from circulation began with great public fires watched by thousands. The first burning of

100,000 shares owned by the King and 300,000 owned by the company took place outside the town hall. In the following weeks, thousands of livres' worth of notes and shares were put into iron cages and burned. All this was aimed at reducing the paper system and partly bringing back the coin-based one. While no one in France had any money, the Regent's mother joked, they had plenty of toilet paper.

But when confidence is lost, it is hard to regain, and this was not the way to bring it back. Every fire further reduced the confidence in paper, and the demand for coins grew stronger. The poor could only hunt in the streets for coins, or exchange goods to feed themselves.

While the poor suffered, the rich in their grand houses and palaces continued to dance. Protected by credit, which no supplier dared deny them, they lived more and more wildly, as if spending would keep the dangers away. In 1720 ten times more was spent at the theatre than in the previous year, people dressed even more richly and ate dinners with dozens of courses.

For the foreign investors who held French banknotes the situation was particularly bad. Their losses increased when the French exchange price dropped even more than the share price. An English pound, worth 39 livres in May, was worth 92 livres by September, and livres could not be exchanged for the next three months. One foreigner who managed to profit from the falling value of French money was Law's friend and former business partner Richard Cantillon, who had returned to Paris in search of further investment opportunities. With a greater ability to see ahead than all the other financiers, he expected the French money to lose value and by various dealings across countries he made a second fortune. The size of some of these deals, which pushed the livre down further, came to Law's attention. There is a story that Law paid a visit to Cantillon's office and said, 'If we were in England we would be able to talk and reach an agreement, but in France, as you know, I can tell you that you will be in the Bastille prison this evening if you do not leave the country in forty-eight hours.' Cantillon left Paris for London, where he turned his attention to South Sea shares – and made another enormous fortune.

◆

At the bank, the fires and the control had done nothing to improve matters. Coin supplies were still too low, even after quantities of coins had been made from other metals apart from gold and silver. Bank openings became shorter and less frequent, and the queues continued to grow. When the doors did open, the competition to get to the front of the line was wild. Everyone thought that the bank would stop payment again in a few days, so the demand for the money was great. People risked their lives to get some coins. One day the guards were forced to shoot at the crowd, killing three people, to keep order. This was just the beginning.

On 17 July, at 3 a.m., a crowd of about 15,000 people gathered in the streets outside the bank. Word had spread that, for the first time in over a week, 10-livre notes would be exchanged for coins between nine and one that morning. Wooden fences had been put up to control the crowd, but no one had expected so many people. At five o'clock several workmen, drunk and tired of waiting, climbed over the fences and tried to get to the front of the queue. From every direction people started to push towards the bank, and those at the front were trapped. By dawn a dozen or more people had died, squeezed to death against the fences or under the feet of the crowd.

A large, angry crowd carried three bodies to the royal palace, and demanded the Regent's attention from outside the locked gates. While the Regent sent for soldiers – there were about 6,000 camped just outside Paris – the Secretary of State and the

Governor of Paris arrived at the palace. As the gates opened to let them in, a crowd of four or five thousand flooded inside. Still in his carriage, the Governor threw handfuls of silver and gold into the crowd to quieten them. Minutes later, his sleeves were torn to bits. The Secretary of State needed guards to help him reach the steps of the palace and face the crowd. Eventually, after a promise that money would be given out around the city, the crowd began to slowly leave.

But the mood in the streets remained ugly. A second crowd directed their attentions to Law and marched to the place Vendôme to hang him. They could not force open the gates to his home, but they threw stones and broke all his windows before the guards arrived and arrested the leaders. Law had heard the noise and wisely escaped to the royal palace. Later that morning Law's empty carriage was seen in the rue Richelieu, leaving a side entrance of the palace. A group blocked its path and attacked. Law's driver suffered cuts and a broken leg before he escaped; the carriage was wrecked.

For his own protection Law moved into the palace. He was deeply shaken by the violence and, as before, the signs of tension were clear. The Regent's mother said he remained 'as white as a sheet' for several weeks after the event. Even when he returned to his own house, the risk of attack remained. Youths, said to be employed by his growing band of enemies, watched him all the time, hoping for a chance for revenge. The children were still at Bourbon's country house, but Katherine was now practically a prisoner in her own house and the hatred with which Law and she were viewed was very frightening. Guards on foot and horseback surrounded their house and the bank's offices day and night. Law always went out with guards and not in his own carriage; he was taking great care.

Parliament was meeting. They were supposed to be considering increasing the trading rights of the Mississippi in return for a large payment. But blaming the troubles on Law's system, the members took advantage of the difficult situation and refused to agree to the arrangement. They hoped that their refusal, added to the trouble in the city, would mean the end of Law. But the Regent struck back and sent them to a village sixty kilometres from Paris. Shareholders saw this as a move to support Law and the share prices rose a little. But the recovery was short, soon overshadowed by frightening news: France faced the plague.

It started in Marseille when crew members on a ship from Syria, where the disease was common, avoided the strict controls and docked in the port. The crew was found to be infected only after they had unloaded their goods. Eight people in the dirty huts surrounding the port suddenly caught the disease. Slowly it spread from the crowded dockside to the grand houses of the rich. Defoe wrote that the illness began with a light pain in the head; then a cold shaking followed, which ended in death. 'And,' he continued, '(which is more terrible) we are informed that not one person, no not one ... touched with it, has been known to recover, and they seldom live above six hours after they are first taken.'

At the end of July, the plague was formally recognized and people were forbidden to enter or leave the city. Supplies of food could not reach the desperate people inside. As the plague spread, the piles of bodies were so high that slaves were brought in to bury them. By August, a third of the citizens – around 15,000 people – had died of hunger or disease. And the plague had spread beyond the city into Provence. In Toulon about 9,000 people died, and 7,500 more in Aix. From there, Defoe said, many people ran into the mountains, hoping that the sharpness of the air in the hills, which were always covered with snow, might save them from the infection.

Europe watched sympathetically but with growing fears that the plague would reach Paris, the Netherlands and even London. 'Large collections have been made ... for the people at Marseille and other places,' reported Defoe, and he specially mentioned the city of Genoa, which sent both money and a ship with food and medical supplies. Law and the Regent also sent large sums to help.

To stop the spread of the plague, strict controls were put in place. Ships were delayed for weeks. In one extraordinary example in Holland, three ships arriving from the East were burned and their crews were forced to come to the shore with no clothes on and to spend a period of time apart on an island. Private travellers had to get health certificates stamped in every town through which they passed.

In many people's minds the plague was like the economic troubles and Law, whose projects had caused the speculation disease, was blamed. The plague destroyed Law's system. The important ports of Marseille and Toulon shut down; trade with Africa and the rest of the Mediterranean stopped. Much of the income of the Mississippi Company stopped too. 'One cannot say what effect the demand for silver had but every ... man sold some of his shares to have enough to feed his family,' Law later wrote. By the time the plague was over it had taken 100,000 lives and, as Law had feared, the system he had created.

Chapter 9   Disaster

Poison against Law spread through Europe. There were dozens of writings which criticized him; there were attacks in poems, plays and paintings, in novels and on playing cards that circulated in bars, coffee-houses and meeting-places in every town and city in Europe. There was even a series of silver coins, which represented Law in the metal he had tried so hard to forbid.

Law could turn his eyes from these attacks, but he could not ignore their existence, nor that they came from pure public hatred. For a man who had always intended to do good, who had

had dreams of bringing happiness to all, the public criticism was deeply hurtful. His behaviour became strange. One day he was full of his old confidence, persuading others and himself that the economy was improving, that it was under control, and telling friends that he would always be the master of all the money in Europe. The next day he was full of doubt, unusually bad-tempered with the members of the council, introducing stricter laws to bring the system back under control. Occasionally, he seemed overcome by responsibilities. Remembering a day spent alone in his apartment in the royal palace, when members of the royal family were out of town and no one was allowed in, he wrote that someone would be less unhappy shut in an infected town like Marseille than in Paris surrounded by people, as he usually was.

He gave even more time to his work. Six hundred workmen were employed to build a new factory to produce coins – probably in the expectation that by the time it was complete there would be enough metal to make them.

To build up his good name, Law published an unsigned defence of his system. When he came to France, he said, the country had been 2 billion livres in debt. Now, thanks to the Mississippi Company and other changes, France was much stronger financially. Readers of this cleverly argued defence were made angry by the fact that it did not mention the present economic difficulties. Inflation, the devaluation of banknotes and shares, the lack of coins and the damage to investors were completely ignored. Pulteney said it was very badly timed because it pretended to show that people were richer and happier, when in fact they were complaining, with good reasons, of poverty and ruin.

Law turned quietly for help to the one man whose financial skill he deeply respected: his old friend, Richard Cantillon. Since Cantillon had left France, the two men had become friends again, and Law had been using Cantillon's services in Amsterdam. Now, with his system failing, Law offered Cantillon great rewards to come and help him sort out the mess. We do not know exactly what rewards were offered, but Cantillon considered the offer carefully and asked his friends' advice. Eventually, realizing the dangers of Law's situation, he refused. Law was not discouraged at first, and sent more persuasive letters to Holland. But when Cantillon refused to change his mind, Law became angry. If Cantillon did not accept the offer, the French would not pay him for the metal he had sent for the company from Amsterdam. It shows how much pressure Law was under that he felt forced to act in such an unprincipled manner. In fact, it was useless to threaten a clever man like Cantillon – it only made him even more certain to stay away.

Law was rapidly becoming an embarrassment that the Regent could not afford. He too was criticized because of Law, and he felt uncharacteristically sensitive to the flood of criticism and hatred. Accusations of murder had been directed against him; his mother had been threatened and advised to poison her own son. In the past he had not cared, but now these things began to worry him. One particularly nasty play made him so angry that he offered a reward of 100,000 livres for the name of the author. But he did not get it, only a couple more rude lines:

You promise much, O Regent.
Is it in paper or silver?

Real economic recovery, the Regent now felt, would never take place while people could not trust Law and his paper system, and while parliament, the financiers and the wealthy were so opposed to Law. Secretly the Regent began to look for help, approaching private bankers and financiers in the hope that they would offer him metal money. Their reaction was not what he hoped. Although they wanted to have a good relationship with the Regent, they knew that a loan might help save Law. They gave no financial assistance, only their usual advice that all the problems would be solved with a return to the old system of money.

On 15 September, Law's career fell to new depths with the publishing of one of his most hated laws. 'The pen falls from one's hands and words fail to explain the measures of this law. Poison was in its tail,' wrote the lawyer Marais as he looked carefully at the new rules. These stated that large notes would soon stop being acceptable money; that all banknotes could only be used if 50 per cent of the payment was in coins; that bank accounts would be reduced to a quarter of their present value, and shares fixed at 2,000 livres. This meant, said Marais, 'bankruptcy of three-quarters of the bank and five-sixths of the Mississippi Company.'

Economic historians still argue about whether the law was in fact Law's idea or whether it was the result of the Regent's meetings with the financiers. It is clear, though, that the public believed the ideas were Law's and blamed him for their suffering. Marais wrote that there was desperation in every family. 'They have to pay for half of everything in coins and there aren't any . . . everything is going up in price instead of coming down.'

The rising inflation was made worse by aristocrats and traders who formed groups, gathered piles of basic goods, and then sold them at high prices. Some of the worst offenders were Law's supporters. Pulteney wrote that d'Estrées had the coffee, Mr William Law some metal, others had the sugar, and the Duc de la Force had the wax. Law knew that this was going on, but did not want to lose his few remaining friends and so ignored it. The Regent did the same. When traders came to complain about the reduction of their bank accounts, he accused them coldly of charging high prices for the past year. One man replied that his business would be destroyed and Orléans answered, 'I am delighted.'

The new law was painful not just to French citizens but also to countless foreigners who traded with France. Groups of traders from Savoy, Piedmont and Brussels came to complain. They had supplied France with enormous quantities of materials and had been paid in French banknotes, which were losing their value and desirability. For English investors, developments were even more tragic. London was in shock from the effects of the crash of South Sea shares. These had reached a high of £1,050 in June, then had dropped at the end of August, and by the middle of September were trading at £380. Investors who had borrowed heavily to buy South Sea shares at high prices, expecting that their value would continue to rise, were now forced to sell other investments to repay their loans. European markets in France, Holland and other countries were damaged by the effect of this disaster.

Through all the confusion, anger and suffering, Law and his family were increasingly criticized. This famous family, who had danced at Versailles and had their hands kissed by international leaders, now lived constantly in the shadow of danger. The lawyer Barbier saw Law's wife and ten-year-old daughter Kate returning home in a carriage pulled by six horses. The carriage was recognized and surrounded by a crowd shouting and swearing and throwing stones at the women. Before the driver could whip the frightened horses and drive away, Kate was struck by a stone and injured.

In the tense atmosphere anyone who even looked like a member of the Law family could find themselves in great danger. Madame de Torcy, the wife of the Foreign Secretary, was half drowned in a pool before she persuaded her attackers that she was not Katherine. During an argument between two carriage drivers in the rue St Antoine, one untruthfully claimed that the passenger inside the other's carriage was Law. Within minutes a crowd had gathered and attacked the innocent passenger, who only escaped with his life by running to safety in a church.

There is annoyingly little to tell us how Katherine reacted to this change in Law's fortune. We can only guess from the loving letters that Law later wrote to her that she remained supportive but increasingly frightened by the political situation that threatened her family's safety. After the attack on her daughter she rarely went out, and then often dressed as a woman expecting a baby – a serious embarrassment for a woman who had always been noted for her fashion sense. Social calls were not only dangerous but could often be insulting. Growing numbers of doors closed in her face. When she visited Madame de Lauzan, an ageing aristocrat famous for her sense of humour, the old lady made fun of her: 'My God, Madame, you have done us a great honour with this visit. We know the risks [with a population that is] against you *for no reason.*' A few friends remained loyal. The Duc de Bourbon continued to offer the family safety at his country house in St Maur when it was feared that the crowd might attack their home. The artist Rosalba Carriera still visited long after most fashionable callers had left and, unlike her relative Pellegrini, who had been paid a little money for painting the ceiling of the bank but wanted more, Rosalba never chased the Laws for money.

The final blow to Law's weakened system came on 10 October with another cruel, but by this stage expected, rule. Since no one now had any confidence in the failing paper money system, from 1 November France would again depend completely on metal coins. Holders of banknotes were forced to exchange them for annual payments. Law's rivals had finally persuaded the Regent. When he heard the news Voltaire remarked that paper was now back to its real value, but Marais' reaction was more emotional: he wrote that this was the end of the system of paper money, which had made a thousand beggars rich and a hundred thousand honest men poor. When the bank finally closed its doors on 27 November, few people were sad.

Mississippi shareholders worried about the news that the bank was going to close, and Law's newly powerful enemies were quick to take revenge against speculators who had profited earlier. Profit as a result of speculation was now seen as criminal. The new law-makers particularly hated the poor investors who had made fortunes – the 'thousand beggars' to whom Marais had referred. Now the winners would become losers.

So that the speculators could be recognized, investors were ordered to bring their shares to the offices of the now closed bank to have them checked. Any unchecked share certificates would be worthless. If no proof of criminal dealing was discovered, the shares would be returned after one week. People who were found guilty of illegal moneymaking would be punished by losing a large percentage of their property. It was a process of revenge.

While it was going on, the share market was shut down. When this news was announced, Marais visited the place. The reaction he remembered was one of shock and horror. Faces changed. It seemed like a defeat, like a battle had been lost. With thousands of others he took his shares to the bank, and was alarmed at the long and confusing process. After endless form-filling and rubber-stamping, he wrote, you took away only a small unsigned piece of paper, on which was your name, the number of your shares and the page in the record. There was a lot of protest at this process, which had not been mentioned in the new rule, but finally all the shareholders had to go through it. The market was crowded and no one knew what was going to happen.

Many people were so afraid of the investigation that they packed their bags with as much wealth as they could squeeze in and made immediate preparations to leave France. At least four important members of Law's staff escaped, fearing that they would be carefully investigated. Vernezobre, one of the head clerks of the bank, went to Holland, taking several millions that belonged to him and others. Angelini, Law's Italian secretary, appeared in black clothes, informed Law that his father had died and begged for permission to go to Italy. He never returned, spending his remaining years in comfort on the income from the money he had invested in property in the Roman countryside.

Though terrible, this fall did not mark the end of the Mississippi Company. Law's enemies, who had tried for months to destroy his complicated company, now rushed to pick out the best bits for themselves. The rights to the incomes from the coin factory and taxes were their first goals. The company, like every other business in the land, was short of cash. To repay various loans and continue to trade, money was urgently needed and further strong action was considered necessary. At the end of November, a new order ruled that every shareholder would have to lend the company 150 livres per share; two-thirds of this amount had to be paid in coins, one-third in paper, which was still in limited circulation because there were so few coins. The shares of anyone who failed to pay would be lost. Again, this was news of the very worst kind for investors. Pulteney wrote sadly that very many investors would not be able to pay because all their wealth was in shares; and that many who were able to pay would choose instead to give up their shares.

Overcome by blame, Law remained alone and depressed in his home, with only Katherine to comfort him. Even she, however, could not keep from him the realization that, now the bank was closed and the company was failing, his position was no longer possible. He offered to give up his official post and asked for permission to leave the country. The Regent, who was waiting to see what would happen next, ignored him. Once again Law was a guilty man, waiting for his punishment to be announced.

With Katherine's help he passed his time trying to organize

his personal financial affairs. During the past weeks, these had become hopelessly mixed up with those of the company. Law was still a kind man, and when an investor told him a sad story he always offered to help. Many of the financial problems that he had after this came from the personal credit notes he gave at this time to poor investors to make up for their losses.

On the surface he could still show the old confidence in himself. When he was told of his enemies' closeness to the Regent he replied, 'The Regent only follows this course to amuse himself, he takes pleasure from it.' Marais watched when Law dared to go out to see the checking of shares. Law arrived at the company offices on 21 November in the middle of the crowds bringing in their shares. He was called a thief and a criminal, wrote Marais: 'He carried his head as high as possible, and everyone wanted him to hang it low.' But ten days later, in early December, Law's spirit was down again. There were signs that parliament's return was coming closer and that, as Law feared, their agreement to cooperate was based on the understanding that he would be arrested. Giving in to pressure from the people who wanted to see Law punished, the Regent continued to ignore his repeated, and increasingly urgent, requests to be allowed to leave the country. By 10 December, the talk was that Law had been arrested, or sacked, and sent to his property at Effiat. Marais, watching more closely, knew that he still had not been given permission to leave the capital but saw the tension becoming clear: Law was in a state of great unhappiness. A terrible storm was coming, and the results would soon be seen. Everyone was getting ready to punish Law, and even in the bank there was talk against him and the Regent.

With tensions rising hourly, Law again asked for a meeting with the Regent but was told he was too ill to see him, an excuse which meant that arrest was near. A day later, the movement to bring Law down grew stronger. There was no doubt that this time he would fall; his enemies were so well organized, said Marais, and included not only the usual group of parliament, financiers and aristocrats against Law but also Madame de Parabère, the Regent's lover, who had said she would only return to his bed if Law was sacked. According to Marais, the Regent was running after her 'like a child'. Faced with such opposition, even Law's most loyal supporter, the Duc de Bourbon, agreed that Law would have to go. The only remaining question was how he would be got rid of and, more importantly, whether his life could be saved.

Encouraged by the Duc de Bourbon, Orléans agreed at last that he would have to act, and quickly. Law finally got his meeting and suggested that the councillor Le Pelletier de la Houssaye should be made Controller General of Finance, to help guide the country out of the economic difficulties. The Regent was not persuaded, reportedly telling the council, 'He did not see among the French anyone who had enough intelligence [to follow Law] in the position with a better chance of success.' De la Houssaye agreed to take the job but not while Law remained in Paris, and suggested that he should be sent to the Bastille prison. Orléans ignored this suggestion and instructed Law to prepare to leave. The British official Sutton noted a sudden burst of activity: '[Law] goes to see those with whom he has business, he receives people at his home with as much if not more freedom than before. He works on settling his accounts, he gives all the explanations asked of him.'

When the new stage production of *Thésée* opened on 12 December, there was general surprise when the theatre-goers realized that the Duc de la Force's group included John Law, Katherine and their children. (The children, one writer admitted, were 'fairly handsomely made'.) It seemed to the observers like 'English pride' to appear so boldly in public at such a moment. Law the over-confident, charming gambler had, it seemed, returned.

In fact, this was Law's goodbye to Paris. Earlier that day, he had had a final meeting with the Regent. The meeting had been very emotional. Law admitted that he had committed many faults. But he claimed he had committed them because he was a man, and all men made mistakes. He promised the Regent most seriously that none of the mistakes had come from dishonest intentions. Law left Paris with his son John on 14 December, heading for his country house Guermande, near Brie, one of many wonderful properties he had bought but had rarely had time to visit. He planned to wait there for a few days until passports arrived allowing him to leave the country. Katherine and Kate stayed in Paris to settle debts, but he expected them to follow soon. Two days later, parliament was recalled.

Chapter 10   Exile and End

Law's feelings for the Regent had not changed. From Guermande he wrote that it was difficult to decide between the desire that he had to retire from public life and the desire he would always have to add to the Regent's greatness. He added, 'when you believe that my opinions could be useful, I will give them freely.'

Law's royal friends seemed equally sad at his departure. Bourbon sent an emotional letter of goodbye. He wrote that he could not express his great sadness on Law's departure. 'I hope that you do not doubt it . . . I will never allow any attack on your freedom or your property. I have the Regent's word on this.' Law was encouraged by the letter – Bourbon and the Regent's support was his only defence against the men who wanted him arrested. In reality, both Bourbon and the Regent were keen to protect Law from his enemies because only Law knew exactly how much money had been printed and where it had all gone. If he were arrested, they too might be found guilty. Making sure of Law's safe exile, and preferably his disappearance from France, was as much in their interests as in his. As Guermande was within easy reach of the capital, Law, also conscious of the danger, begged Bourbon for a passport. His departure would be in the national interest, he argued: 'Perhaps my distance will soften [my enemies], and time will make them realize the purity of my intentions.'

On the morning of his first day in exile, the English official Crawford arrived unannounced. The English, always interested in Law's brilliant career, were curious about his sudden fall. Crawford found Law in reasonable spirits and wanted to learn as much as possible about his downfall. With the excuse of discussing a debt, Crawford invited himself to stay for a few days. Law welcomed his visit – talking was helpful and, more importantly, allowed him to be sure that the British government would hear his side of the story.

In long conversations over the next two days Law talked about his career in France. He was still full of confidence, did not apologize for his actions, and was very proud that the Regent had already told him that he did not need to distance himself too far, and that he could depend on his friendship and on his protection against enemies. When Crawford asked him about his future plans, Law suggested that he would not stay in France much longer. He wanted the Regent's permission to have returned to him the 500,000 livres he had originally brought with him from Holland and to be allowed to go to Rome.

Soon after Crawford had gone back to Paris to write down all he had learned, the aristocrat de Lassay and Bourbon's secretary arrived, bringing with them, on the orders of the Duc de Bourbon, the passports Law had requested and a large sum of money he had not expected. Law was thankful for the passports but refused the money, saying that he already had enough for his journey and the immediate future. Later he recalled that he had with him 800 gold coins and a diamond or two. He expected that, as Bourbon and the Regent had promised, the rest of his money would be sent when his accounts were settled. There seemed no reason to doubt their promise. It was a misjudgement that he would regret for the rest of his life.

Preparations to leave France were made rapidly. With enemies shouting for his arrest he had to travel in secret, and it was impossible therefore to use his own carriages. Bourbon gave him two carriages – one of his own and one belonging to his lover, the beautiful Madame de Prie.

Law left Guermande on the evening of 17 December. He was with his son, three servants and several of the Duke's guards, who wore long, grey coats over their uniforms to avoid being recognized. He had two passports, one in the name of du Jardin, the other in his real name, and several letters from friends, including one from the Duke guaranteeing his safe journey. The escape route, planned by Bourbon so that fresh horses were waiting where necessary, passed north of Paris towards St Quentin, Valenciennes and across the border with Flanders to Mons and Brussels.

Despite the careful preparations, the plan went wrong. The group was stopped at the border by a local official who, unluckily for Law, was the eldest son of his old enemy, d'Argenson. The official's confusion at the false passports turned to joy when he realized who the passengers really were. In revenge for his father's fall, he 'refused absolutely' to allow Law to pass and pretended that the passports had been stolen. He took Law's money and the Duke's letter and held them while a message was sent to Paris. 'I made Law very frightened, I arrested him and held him for twenty-four hours, only letting him go when I received formal orders from the court,' he said later. When Law asked for his money, d'Argenson refused to return it, reminding Law that it was illegal to take gold abroad — according to a rule introduced by Law himself.

Law arrived in Brussels exhausted, frightened, but glad to have escaped. It proved impossible for him to live secretly. Brussels treated him as an important visitor. He spent the first morning in a meeting with the French ambassador, de Prie, the husband of Bourbon's fashionable lover, and attended a grand dinner that evening at which the high society of Brussels was present. The next night he went to the theatre and as he entered everyone stood and clapped. 'This,' the English official Sutton remarked, 'attracts attention'.

Back in Paris the talk was of 'an amazing number of carriages filled with gold and silver' that had also been sent across the border to Flanders. There were many theories about this money. Some said it was for buying political support; some said it was part of the marriage settlement of the Duc de Chartres; some said it was a private store for the Regent to retire on when the King started to govern. On one thing everyone agreed: that the Regent's representative lacked nothing. In England similar accusations appeared in the press. The accusations of stealing French money lasted for years and caused Law great heartache. His letters to Bourbon, Orléans and de Lassay are filled with countless explanations and claims of innocence.

In Brussels Law felt uncomfortable and he decided to move on as quickly as he could. But since his money had been lost at the border, he spent the next two days raising money, either through loans or gambling, before continuing the journey south. Crossing the Alps in the middle of winter was very dangerous, but by 21 January Law and his son had arrived in Venice. They saw no one for a few days. 'I have suffered terribly from the voyage,' he admitted to de Lassay, in one of the first letters he wrote after his arrival.

Law felt he could make no firm decisions about the future

until money was sent and Katherine and his daughter joined him. Over the following weeks, as he waited impatiently for news from France, he settled into city life. The entertainments in Venice made him miss Katherine and his daughter even more. He wrote sadly to Kate: 'We often think of you, your brother and I, and wish you were here with Madame ... I hope to see you again soon, until then your main duty must be to please Madame, and to soften the pain that she has in my affairs.'

Money had still not arrived and he depended on friends like de Lassay, who lent him £30,000, and on gambling to provide enough money to live on and pay off his endless debts. 'Last year I was the richest man there ever was and today I have nothing.' The old gambling skills, based on his knowledge of probability, were quickly practised. A friend from Paris described him as playing 'from morning to night. He is always happy when gambling.' Each day Law suggested new games. After one specially profitable game he was said to have made 20,000 livres at cards. But on several other occasions there are references in his letters to losses he could not afford.

Away from the gambling tables he wrote increasingly urgent letters to the Regent and Bourbon, begging them to send, as promised, the 500,000 livres he had brought with him to France. All his other shares and properties, worth about 100 million livres, he willingly gave to the company to pay his debts and help those who had lost most during the system's downfall.

When it arrived, the news from Paris was alarming. De la Houssaye had reported to a council meeting that 2.7 billion livres in bank accounts, notes and other forms of debt guaranteed by the King were still unpaid and there was no hope of repaying them. The Regent and Bourbon rushed to distance themselves publicly from Law, and each tried to blame the other for allowing him to escape. The Pâris brothers were recalled from exile to run the investigation into the bank. The effects of Law's system became clear when half a million people came forward with claims for losses as a result of his shares and banknotes. Nearly two hundred investors had to pay a total of almost 200 million livres as a punishment for speculation – the Widow Chaumont paid 8 million livres, but remained rich because she had wisely put so much money into property. 'Those who have lost are already ruined, and now they wish to ruin those who gained,' wrote a journalist.

The Mississippi Company was also investigated and the shares decreased from 135,000 to 56,000. In this weakened state the company lasted until the end of the eighteenth century. In all the financial confusion, Law was conveniently blamed for everything, and was accused of stealing and of leaving enormous unsettled debts. A later document sent to the Duc de Bourbon showed that in fact Law's own account was several millions in credit.

As bad feeling grew against him, and unable to defend himself, Law became increasingly worried about Katherine's safety. In April, when travelling conditions had improved, he instructed her to prepare to leave: 'I want your company and to live as we used to do before,' he wrote. Katherine's preparations to leave were stopped by the investigators. Her request for passports was refused. All Law's properties, including the Hôtel de Langlée, where Katherine was living at the time, were seized. She had to rent rooms, with only two servants to help her. Then, on 8 May, William Law, suspected of planning an escape, was arrested and put in prison. Perhaps to spare him further worry, Katherine did not tell Law what had happened and he still did not know when he wrote disappointedly to her, 'I find you have [no desire] to come to Italy, I agree that England or Holland would be better . . . you may go to Holland.'

A letter from Paris to Venice could take weeks to arrive. When news of the situation in Paris did reach Law, he was shocked. 'Madame Law writes that they find me a debtor of 7 million to the bank, and of 5 or 6 million to the company ... that my brother is in prison ... without being told the reason. You know that I paid no attention to my own interests, that I didn't know the exact state of my affairs; my time was ... taken up with public service.' Now he realized he had only two choices left if he wanted justice: to return to France, or move to England and put pressure on Bourbon and Orléans through his friends at the English court.

Earlier, Law had received a pardon from George I and forgiveness from the Wilsons. To show his loyalty to France, he had given the royal pardon to the Regent. Now Law hoped that the English king would give him another pardon. He claimed he could be helpful to England, but that if he was refused he could go to work for another country. He had certainly received offers from Denmark and Russia, which he had refused. Law had to 'look for a protector to avoid a prison sentence'. The idea of debtors' prison was always present and probably his experience of Newgate prison in his youth made him frightened of returning to one. But when, by late summer, there was still no clear decision and his enemies were growing more threatening, Law decided to risk going to England. He arrived in October; it was the first time he had set foot in England for twenty-six years.

Law's arrival created mixed feelings and was twice discussed in the House of Lords. Some, like Coningsby, attacked Law for the damage he had done in France, for taking French nationality and for changing his religion. Others, like Carteret, supported Law, arguing that he had been pardoned by the King in 1717 and that it was the right of every citizen to return to his native land. By November things had settled down and people were beginning to think that Law could help in the relationship between England and France. Law still wanted to see Katherine and hoped that his move to England might help.

Although Law had been given a small salary by the Regent, and the London bankers had given him limited credit on his accounts, he still struggled to pay his debts. But little by little he was welcomed back into fashionable London society. People wanted to meet him – and were always charmed when they did. In the new year of 1722, he was a regular visitor at court. He spoke frequently with the King, probably in German because George spoke little English. He also spent much of his time quietly, enjoying a regular horse ride with his son. He told Katherine that the exercise made him feel much better.

But the passing months brought little real improvement. He could still be arrested for debt at any time, and Katherine was still refused permission to leave France. Added to these worries, his relationship with his brother William became very difficult. William had written long, complaining letters to him in Venice and had even sent his wife Rebecca, who was expecting a baby, to Venice to beg for help. Law had always tried to help them. However, since he came to England, there had been more quarrels over debts and disagreements about property. Law suggested to a friend that perhaps prison had made his brother mad. But when he learned that some of the talk about his supposed secret fortune outside France had been started by his brother he was very angry.

In October 1723, almost two years after his arrival in England, Law began to make preparations to return to France. On 2 December, exhausted by his lifestyle and the pressures of government, Orléans had a heart attack at the age of forty-nine and died in the arms of one of his lovers. Law's hopes of returning to France died with the Regent, and his salary was stopped.

Desperate for money, worried that he might be thrown into a debtors' prison at any moment, Law turned to Walpole, the head of the British government, for a job. Because of his religion Law was forbidden to hold an official post, but Walpole agreed. Law was delighted. He received his first payment from the government, and crossed the English Channel on 9 August 1725. His role was unusual; he would pretend to be a traveller as he journeyed through Europe, but in reality he would report anything of interest he noticed. At the age of fifty-four, Law had a new career: he was a spy.

Law always enjoyed playing the man of mystery, and he enjoyed his new job. He met some European princes, and then reported their conversations back to London. But a month later he was still waiting for instructions, and he began to suspect that his help was not quite so important to the British as he had expected. He travelled to Augsberg and Munich and took every opportunity to mix in political circles. He met ambassadors and princes, and he waited for instructions from Britain. There was no sign that anyone there paid any attention to his reports.

Eventually Law grew tired of waiting and gave up his job. Venice, the city in which he had always felt at home, called his attention again. In 1726, he returned there for the third and final time. Enemies remained a worry; some had threatened to kill him and his son. Desperate to find a way of leaving something for his family, Law began investing his winnings from gambling in art. Perhaps Katherine helped by sending some of his paintings from Paris before their possessions were seized. Within two years, Law had a collection of nearly 500 works, including paintings by Titian, Raphael, Tintoretto, Veronese, Holbein, Michelangelo, Poussin and Leonardo. Again, Law was showing his highly original business skills. Burges, the English representative in Venice, thought Law had been badly cheated: 'No man alive believes that his pictures when they [are] sold will bring half the money they cost him.' But time has proved Law correct. Today such a collection could be owned only by a very small number of the wealthiest people on earth.

Law's pleasure was mixed with sadness, but until the end few people realized how desperate he was. The famous writer Montesquieu visited him, and Law told him of the early days of the bank and the company. Montesquieu had never been sympathetic to Law, but he found him to be 'more in love with his ideas than his money' and 'still the same man, with little money . . . his mind full of projects, his head full of calculations.'

But even if Montesquieu failed to realize it, Law was deeply changed. When, after seven long years, the investigation of Law's affairs in France still continued, he understood that they would never be settled in his lifetime. He became desperate and his health began to fail. As winter passed, he became seriously ill. He had suffered from a weak chest and repeated fevers for some years. At the end of February, he developed a shaking cold fever which lasted five or six hours, and that was followed by a violent hot fever which did not go away. Death held no fears for him. He told Burges that his death would help his family because then their troubles would finally end. He instructed his 22-year-old son to go to Paris immediately after his death and ask for the King's forgiveness.

Burges and the French ambassador, Gergy, realizing the end was near, stayed with Law, anxious to examine his papers after his death. He had mentioned in earlier letters to France that he was writing a history of his system, and they hoped this document would be found among his papers. It was also thought that the papers would include details of the secret fortune with which everyone still believed he had escaped.

Law made a will in which he left everything to Katherine. He did not mention their children, nor the fact that she was not legally his wife. Two days later, on 21 March 1729, a month before his fifty-eighth birthday, the end came peacefully. 'Mr Law is dead, after struggling seven or eight and twenty days.' The doctors had said from the beginning that this fever would be final. 'He died with great calmness . . . and is spoken of here with much respect,' recorded Burges, whose feelings for the exile had grown over the past years. Less sympathetically, the newspaper the *State of Europe* described Law as 'a gentleman who has made himself so famous in the world by the . . . project of the Mississippi . . . that his name . . . will be remembered to the end of the world.'

Young John Law, who had been at his father's bedside when he died, was very sad. He wrote to Katherine describing Law as both father and friend, and telling her about the will. Gergy sympathetically invited the young man to stay at his house, but he was really more interested in 'the secret paper' and the will than in the boy's suffering. John gave Gergy several of his father's letter books, one of which is now in the Bibliothèque de Méjanes, a library in Aix-en-Provence, but tried to keep the will secret. Gergy, however, managed to make a copy of it, which he sent to Paris.

The day after his death, Law's body was taken to the old church of San Gemignano in the Piazza San Marco and he was buried the next day. Nearly eighty years later, when Venice was under Napoleon's rule, the church was ordered to be destroyed. Luckily, one of the French governors of the city was Law's great-nephew, Alexander Law. He ordered his famous relative's body to be moved to the church of San Moise. Law's grave is still there, near the Exchange where he once passed his days, a suitable resting place for a man who spent so much of his life enjoying the pleasures of the city and who, in the end, became a tourist attraction himself.

◆

Even after his death Law's wishes were not respected. His brother opposed the will and claimed Law's goods for himself, arguing that Katherine and Law were not married and therefore he was

Law's closest relative. French judges decided against Katherine but gave the property to William's children, who had been born in France. One can hardly imagine Katherine's reaction to the news of Law's death and his brother's actions. She had visited and supported William while he was in prison, and had helped her sister-in-law as much as she could. It was a desperately cruel blow to be repaid in such a manner.

In all the sorrow, Katherine gained one advantage from Law's death. As he had expected, his death helped his family; the government dropped all accusations against him and allowed Katherine and her daughter to leave France. Young John had joined the Austrian army, and to be near him his mother settled first in Brussels, then in Utrecht. Tragically, only five years after his father's death, the son caught a fever in Maastricht and died. Katherine sold fifteen paintings and moved into a religious house, where she lived until her death in 1747.

Law's daughter Kate was luckier. She married her cousin, the aristocrat Wallingford, and lived the life of a London society hostess in a grand house in Grosvenor Street. Walpole admired her good looks and remarked how similar she was to her father.

◆

John Law had come to France rich, charming, full of energy and ambition, confident he could create an economic boom. While he seemed to succeed, he had been the people's hero and one of the richest and most powerful men in Europe. In his own eyes he failed not because of any mistakes in his ideas or ability but because of his own impatience: 'I do not pretend that I have not made mistakes, I admit that I have made them, and if I could start again ... I would go more slowly but more carefully.' However, this was only part of the reason for his downfall. He had ignored human nature. He had not imagined how his system would encourage people's desire to make as much money for as little effort as possible; how they would follow the crowd, hide money if threatened, and panic if confidence was shaken. He was destroyed by these basic human characteristics, by powerful enemies, and by the tragic plague.

His paper money and his tax changes were swept away, but the effects of his system remained. The high inflation he had created devalued the State's debt by two-thirds and removed the need for high taxation. France was left with a working economy which allowed the royal family to remain in power for a few more years. The cost was to people who held government debts and Mississippi shares: they were ruined. Banknotes based on the value of land returned eighty years later, and a state bank in the nineteenth century.

Looking back, Law interests us as much for his faults and his innocence as for his brilliance. Over the years, opinion on Law has changed. In the eighteenth century, his failure was remembered more than his ideas. Important economists admitted he was clever but criticized his actions. In the nineteenth century Karl Marx described him slightly more sympathetically as a pleasant mixture of a cheat and a fortune-teller. In the twentieth century, he has mostly been forgotten except by economic historians. J. K. Galbraith, a Harvard economist, writing in the 1970s, said that Law, 'showed, perhaps better than any man since, what a bank could do with and to money.'

Many of Law's ideas, which were new in his time, are normal to us now. Paper money and complicated companies with various interests and types of income were extraordinary then, but are quite ordinary now.

Looking at Law's story three centuries later, one cannot help feeling that nothing has really changed. Today paper and plastic are unthinkingly accepted as valuable, and at the press of a button millions of dollars move around the world. But stock exchanges, banks and economies still fail. We have seen the rapid rise and fall of the Asian economies, Russia's financial breakdown, uncertainty in China and Brazil, the enormous losses created by Nick Leeson at Barings Bank and the speculation fever in Internet company shares. Most amazingly of all, within our information universe, confidence is as important as ever and crowd decisions can still cause frightening changes to markets. John Law would be amazed to see that balancing finances remains as difficult as ever.

Business Wordlist

accountant	a person who reports the finances of a company
bid	an offer to do work, provide a service or pay a particular price for something
branch	part of a large organization, often a shop or an office
capital	money that helps to build a new business
consultant	a person who gives business advice
corporation	a big company
to expand	to increase or grow
expert	a person with special knowledge of a subject
link	a connection or a relationship between people, organizations, ideas or things
loan	money that has been lent
negotiate	to try to come to an agreement with another person
network	a system that connects people, organizations or things together
objective	a business aim
partnership	a business that is owned by two or more people
project	a piece of work that needs knowledge, skill and planning
publish	to print something and offer it for sale to the public
sack	to tell someone to leave their job
share	a piece of paper that says you own a part of a company
stock exchange	a place where people buy and sell shares
trade	to buy and sell

85

ACTIVITIES

Chapters 1–3

Before you read

1 John Law lived from 1671 to 1729. What do you know about this period in history? What was happening in your country at that time?

2 Answer the questions. Find the words in *italics* in your dictionary. They are all in the story.

   a How are these words connected with money?

     account bankrupt credit gamble interest invest

   b How might these words be connected with each other?

     (love) affair aristocrat carriage duel

   c Translate these sentences into your language.

     The *duke* was *exiled* for his crimes to one of Britain's *colonies*. He was *pardoned* twenty years later.

     The *goldsmith* died when *plague* swept through the town.

After you read

3 Which of these statements are true? Correct the false ones.

   a London was the largest Western European capital in the late seventeenth century.

   b Law found a job when he arrived in London.

   c Banking started in 500 BC.

   d The Greeks invented paper money.

   e Law killed Wilson with one blow.

   f The Duke of Shrewsbury helped the Wilsons hunt for Law.

   g Katherine and Law kept their affair a secret.

   h Queen Anne refused to pardon Law.

   i The Darien plan made Scotland a rich country.

4 Work with two other students. Imagine the conversation between Law, Wilson and Wightman in the Fountain bar before the duel. Act out the scene.

Chapters 4–5

Before you read

5   You know some of Law's ideas from his plans for England and Scotland. Chapters 4 and 5 are called 'The Rise of John Law' and 'Success'. What do you think Law did when he went to Europe? How did he become a success?

6   Find the words in *italics* in your dictionary.

   a   Which of these are words for jobs?
       financier   millionaire   regent

   b   Which of these actions involve money?
       arrest   devalue   speculate

   c   When might a person
       –   experience a *boom*?
       –   receive a *dividend*?
       –   *panic*?
       –   be interested in a *short-term* gain?

After you read

7   At this point in the story, if you had been in Paris, would you have been one of Law's friends or one of his enemies? Explain your reasons.

8   Discuss why the following are important to the story.

   a   Law's journey to Paris in 1706
   b   Louis XIV's death in 1715
   c   the share boom in 1719
   d   the number of banknotes printed by the end of 1719

Chapters 6–9

Before you read

9   Look at the chapter titles on the Contents page and imagine what is going to happen in this part of the story. Discuss your ideas with another student.

10   What are the words in *italics* in your language? Check in your dictionary.

a There are no £1 notes in *circulation* in the UK now.

b We are in a period of low *inflation*.

c There are fewer police officers to *investigate* crimes.

After you read

11 Complete this paragraph about the plague. Add as many words in the gaps as you want.

The plague started ...... It spread from ..... to ..... and then out to ..... . People who caught it .... The city of Genoa .... Travellers had to get ...... In the end ..... were dead and Law's system ......

Chapter 10

Before you read

12 Have you changed your mind about being one of Law's friends or one of his enemies? Why?

13 What kind of document is your *will*? Find the word in your dictionary. What is its purpose?

After you read

14 Do you believe Law had a secret fortune? Make a list of points from Chapter 10 that suggest he was rich and another list of points which suggest he was poor.

Writing

15 Write a letter from Law to his mother describing his life during the early years of his first exile, 1695–97. If you know one of the cities he visited, include a description of it in your letter.

16 Imagine you went to the rue Quincampoix to buy shares at the height of the boom. Describe your experiences.

17 You are one of the people kidnapped by the commercial soldiers and sent to Louisiana. Write a diary of your journey and first few months there.

18 Write a letter from Law in Venice in 1726 to the Regent, defending himself against his enemies' accusations and asking for help.

19 Write a letter from Katherine in Paris to Law in Venice. Remember that although she has to give him bad news, she always tries not to worry him.

20 If you had to be one of the characters in this story, who would you choose to be? Why?